S1

Now, Let Me Tell You What I Really Think

This Large Print Book carries the
Seal of Approval of N.A.V.H.

Now, Let Me Tell You What I Really Think

Chris Matthews

Thorndike Press • Waterville, Maine

Published in 2002 by arrangement with The Free Press,
a division of Simon & Schuster, Inc.

Thorndike Press Large Print Nonfiction Series.

The tree indicium is a trademark of Thorndike Press.

The text of this Large Print edition is unabridged.
Other aspects of the book may vary from the original edition.

Set in 16 pt. Plantin by Al Chase.

Printed in the United States on permanent paper.

Library of Congress Cataloging-in-Publication Data
Matthews, Christopher, 1945–
    Now, let me tell you what I really think / Chris Matthews.
        p. cm.
    Originally published: New York : Free Press, c2001.
    ISBN 0-7862-4120-9 (lg. print : hc : alk. paper)
    1. United States — Politics and government — 2001–
2. United States — Politics and government — 1993–2001.
3. Political culture — United States.   4. Popular culture —
United States.   5. Politicians — United States.
6. Celebrities — United States.   7. United States — Social
conditions — 1980–   8. Large type books.   I. Title.
E902 .M38 2002

                                                    2002019908

To Dad

/

ACKNOWLEDGMENTS

There's a memorable line in the 1968 film *Pretty Poison* in which the main character reflects on life's hard-earned wisdom, "I've learned that people only really pay attention to what they discover for themselves." Everything in this book has been learned at a price. It took me until middle age to realize how the American love of country affects our politics. It took a hard look back to realize the full impact of my 1950s Catholic regimen of sin, the flag, and hide-under-your-desk air raid drills. Or how the Vietnam and civil rights conflicts of the 1960s tempered the politics of my youth.

As you read these pages, you will meet the multiple influences on my political thinking. An Irish-American mom; a practical-conservative dad; a liberal-minded English teacher; Richard Nixon; John F. Kennedy; Barry Goldwater; Eugene McCarthy; Edmund Muskie; Jimmy Carter; Thomas P. "Tip" O'Neill, Jr.; Ronald Reagan; a bunch of guys in Africa; and my hero, Winston Churchill, have all gotten into my head and heart.

I realize now that it all started with my family. I have four great brothers, all different. Herb awoke me to history. Jim is my close political compadre. Bruce, who can narrate the Civil War in its entirety, carries the family's patriotic banner, and Charlie reminds me that the here-and-now of human experience comes just once.

I want to thank my three aunts, Eleanor, Agnes, and Catherine, and my godmother, Toby, for praying and rooting for me since I was born.

I must also acknowledge the people who opened the doors for me over the years: Congressman Wayne Owens and Senator Frank Moss of Utah, who welcomed me to Capitol Hill; Bob Schiffer and Richard Sorenson, who ran my congressional campaign in 1974; Florida Speaker of the House Richard Pettigrew, who brought me aboard to work for President Carter; Hendrik Hertzberg, who promoted me to presidential speechwriter; Martin Franks and Congressman Tony Coelho, who introduced me to Speaker O'Neill; Larry Kramer, who hired me for the *San Francisco Examiner*, and Philip Bronstein, who made me a national columnist for the *San Francisco Chronicle*; David Corvo, who hired me as a commentator for *CBS This Morning*; John

McLaughlin, who invited me so many times to the *McLaughlin Group*; Jack Ryan, who made me a very frequent contributor to *Good Morning America*; and Roger Ailes, who gave me a show to host on CNBC.

For the success of *Hardball*, I have to thank Robert Wright, Andrew Lack, Erik Sorenson, Rob Yarin, Adam Levine, Neil Shapiro, and especially the executive producer, Phillip Griffin.

For her diligence in organizing this book I want to thank Meaghan Nolan. For the force and clarity of her editing, I want to thank Michele Slung. For their philosophical insights, I want to thank Noah Oppenheim and Mark Johnson. Thanks to Jill Eynon, my dedicated assistant; to Marc Abernathy and Professor Kenneth Jowitt; to Bill Hatfield, Elizabeth Maloy, and Peter Hamby. And to Elaine Mintzer for her timely help with the manuscript.

Once again I want to thank my editor, Dominick Anfuso, for his courage, enthusiasm, and friendship, and my literary agent and champion, Raphael Sagalyn, who has been my strong partner from the beginning. And a proud salute to my friends at Simon & Schuster and The Free Press: Martha Levin, Carolyn Reidy, Kristen McGuiness, and Michele Jacob.

Most of all, I want to thank my queen, Kathleen, for her love and two decades of editorial brilliance. And Michael, Thomas, and Caroline, for putting up with Dad while he figured out what he really thinks.

CONTENTS

THIS COUNTRY

I liked the way President Harry Truman talked about us. He called us "this country." He didn't mean the government in Washington, but the American people in those splendid moments when we feel and act as one.

Some of those moments I have witnessed firsthand. I was a college freshman when Jack Kennedy was shot, in remote Africa when Americans crossed the star-filled night on their way to the moon. I shared this country's anger at Vietnam, Watergate, and the petty indignities of the Clinton era.

Through it all, I have watched the American spirit not only survive but prevail. Where politicians have failed us, the country itself has always risen to the challenge, quickened at each new assault on its morale.

I write these words in the days just after the World Trade Center horror. I have just heard President Bush say at the National Cathedral that a country, like a person, "discovers" itself in adversity.

I expect we will discover the country of our birth. That first flag of the American revolution showed a coiled snake and the words "Don't Tread On Me."

Japan learned that lesson in 1945, as did Adolf Hitler before him, as will those who attacked our homeland in 2001. This country is an optimistic, upbeat land. For two hundred years we have shown little ambition for foreign conquest, total interest in building and protecting our society here at home.

In the days following September 11, 2001, the optimism of two hundred years began shining through the wreckage. Rejecting the role of the victim, we gave blood, flaunted the flag, rooted for our new president to do what was right.

INTRODUCTION

WHY I INTERRUPT

The big complaint I get about *Hardball* is that I interrupt the guests too much. I hear it from those on the left and those on the right. They all say the same thing, and I've heard it enough to get the message.

Still, when people tell me to shut up and stop interrupting — "What is it, an ego thing with you?" one guy wrote me — I like to remind myself of what my hero Winston Churchill once said about this shared habit of ours: "All the years that I have been in the House of Commons I have always said to myself one thing: Do Not Interrupt! and I have never been able to keep that resolution."

The truth is, I can come up with some explanations for this oft-cited "bad" habit of mine. There's the TV excuse: I refuse to let plodding guests kill my *Hardball* pace. I like it fast. So does the audience — and probably even, secretly, some of those who complain do too. Or there's the professional rationale: I'm not in the PR business. I'm a journalist. Therefore, I refuse to let politicians use my show to recite their staff-scripted talking points.

I could also offer the "I-grew-up-in-a-big-family" dodge. With five brothers around the table, we had to eat fast to get second helpings — and talk fast in order to get anyone to listen.

But are you ready for the real reason I interrupt so much? I can't help myself.

It's like that Phil Ochs song from the sixties, when he declared, "I've got something to say and I'm gonna say it now." That's me. A guest will say something, and suddenly I'll be reminded of something I'm dying to say.

This book is a chance to finally get it out, to tell you what I really think.

I understand the risks. I know a lot of people have a lot of theories about my politics and where I really stand. They seem to need to know, with all the philosophical ends neatly tied up, whether I'm a liberal or a conservative.

Well, with this book I'm forfeiting my *Miranda* rights: *Everything* I say will be used against me.

I certainly don't expect or want you to like everything I confess here. Like Bogie's Sam Spade in *The Maltese Falcon*, "a little trouble I don't mind." And I'm hoping the act of exhausting my passions in print may release some of the pressure I feel to interrupt while on the air. Maybe it will stop me from repeating the same old brilliant observations that my queen, Kathleen, has been listening to at dinnertime for two decades and restore novelty to my dinnertime diatribes.

What you'll read here is what you'd get if you were sitting across the table from me. I have spent much of my life on a political odyssey. Born to a Republican family, I cried with Richard Nixon and was attracted to the libertarianism of Barry Goldwater. Then came Dallas, civil rights, Vietnam, the draft, and "the sixties." I even found a new Democratic hero, Eugene McCarthy, and fell into the grip of a wild new adventure, Africa.

I have many stories to tell. Like others of my post–WW II generation, I spent my early school years hiding under my desk counting the fifteen minutes it would take for the A-bombs to drop, an experience that may or may not explain my premature interest in politics. I spent two years as a Peace Corps volunteer in the remote southern African kingdom of Swaziland.

Back home I got my first job in politics, guarding the Pentagon Papers and other assignments with the U.S. Capitol Police. I worked for a couple of U.S. senators and ran for the U.S. Congress as a maverick Democrat against Philadelphia's old political machine. I served in the White House for four years with Jimmy Carter, including two years writing his speeches. I spent six years as a top aide to House Speaker Tip O'Neill. I covered the fall of the Berlin Wall, the dissolution of the Iron Curtain, and the first all-races election in South Africa.

I now spend five nights a week talking to some of the most powerful people in this country, and many of the most fascinating as well. Whoever they are, it's my job to get them to come clean. I want to know what they *really* think.

But if you've ever watched me and wondered what *I* really think — you're about to find out.

CHAPTER ONE

AN AMERICAN ATTITUDE

It was October 18, 2000, the morning after the third and final Gore-Bush debate. I was invited on the *Today* show to offer my political analysis of who had won. Gore had already declared his previous night's performance to be his "Goldilocks" debate: "The first was too hot. The second was too cool. The third was just right." And his fairytale verdict had gone unchallenged by the media. Until Matt Lauer asked me what I thought.

Here's what I said: "I think Gore was more aggressive last night, and if you look at the polls, he won on a couple of points. But clearly the interesting question again is, Who do you like? *Bush* won."

Matt Lauer leaped on me like a cougar from a tree: "Let's be honest here, you've been saying that all along. Al Gore *irritates* you."

Me: "The public has been saying that too."

Matt (a second time): "Al Gore *irritates* you."

Me (again): "The public has been saying that too."

Matt: "But you just don't like Al Gore's style, and it's very hard for you to look past it."

Me: "No, no. I think the interesting thing is — I've been studying this election for about a year now — the economy *should* get the incumbent elected. Gore should win. The issue agenda — prescription drugs and those kinds of issues — are all working for the incumbent administration. So what's stopping the American people? There's some tissue rejection there about Al Gore, something that stops them from saying, 'Okay . . . Gore.' I think the American people have a problem with him."

Matt: "So let's be clear . . ."

Me: "They may resolve it. They may say he's better than the other guy."

Matt: "But the American people also haven't taken to George W. Bush."

Me: "That's true, because he's not prepared to be president in many ways."

Matt: "Well, that's a pretty bold statement you just said."

Me: "I think there's a problem between a guy they know who loves government too much and a guy who doesn't know government too much. And they have to choose between two very incomplete candidates. This is not the heavyweight championship here."

Matt Lauer's resistance to my verdict confirmed what I had suspected walking into 30 Rockefeller Plaza that morning. The media cognoscenti had made their call: Gore had not only won, he had cleaned Bush's clock! For Matt certainly was not alone in his thinking. *The New York Times* ruled that the Democratic candidate "dominated" the debate. Its lead editorial called Gore the "aggressor and pace-setter" of the evening who "seemed to throw Mr. Bush off balance." *The Washington Post*'s Tom Shales, the top TV columnist in the country, called it Gore's "best performance." *Times* columnist William Safire, a conservative, agreed that Gore "came on strong." Soon, the internal buzz at NBC was that I had been expressing opinion rather than analysis. The implication was that I was being biased. How could anyone who had declared that George W. had "won" that debate not be?

I'll tell you how.

Right after Gore's "Goldilocks" performance, pollster Frank Luntz, who MSNBC had hired for the 2000 election, met with thirty-six "undecided" voters. Thirty of those thirty-six "liked" George Bush better than his rival. A Gallup Poll taken immediately after the debate found that slightly more people (46 to 44 percent) judged Gore the better debater. But, by 60 to 31 percent — two to one! — they said Bush was more "likeable." By the same two-to-one ratio, the public judged Gore to be the "unfair" debater. Bush also was viewed as more "believable" than Gore.

Watching the night before, I, too, thought Gore had turned in his best performance. But after seeing the reactions from the Luntz focus group and the Gallup Poll I realized that Gore's reflexive arrogance, which I had witnessed personally so many times before, was now, after three primetime exposures, turning off the heartland voter. Matt was right. Gore's negative campaigning had long irritated me. The polling now told me it was also irritating much of the country.

The reason Bush is the president today is simple: When millions of voters saw Al Gore campaigning and in the debates, they took away an impression of negativity and condescension. They decided that they would have to go with the unproven, as Gore would say, "risky" alternative. The debate audience preferred the notion of having a guy in the White House who often spoke English as if it were his second language to one who spoke to us as if English were *our* second language.

It turned out that George W. Bush "won" that debate even more decisively than, forty years earlier, Jack Kennedy had beaten Richard Nixon. The proof was in the polls. Gore led Bush by 47 to 44 percent in the Gallup during the thirty days prior to the debates. He fell behind Bush 47 to 43 percent in the fifteen days after.

The Gore people had thought their man's performance in the third debate would be the deal maker. With the strong economy at his back, the Democratic vice-president would overtake the rival he and much of the media dismissed as a know-nothing frat boy and go on to score a clear-cut victory in November.

They were wrong. The candidate with the undeniable bragging rights on the economic front tripped over his own I-know-best personality. The debates for which Gore had lusted ended up giving Bush the momentum. Had the Texas governor not suf-

23

fered a pair of postdebate stumbles — an out-of-the-past leak of an old driving-under-the-influence charge and a lamebrained claim that Social Security was not a federal program — he would have ridden that Big Mo right through to election day.

Instead, Bush lost the popular vote, needed the intervention of the Supreme Court to win in the Electoral College, and inherited a country that would remain as politically divided as it had shown itself that first week in November 2000.

HERE'S WHAT I REALLY THINK: Al Gore lost one presidential election and may well lose another because of who he is and who we are. I think there's such a thing as an American *attitude*. It manifests itself in the candidates we like and in those we don't. Just as a human being possesses a soul as well as a body, this country has a *spirit* as well as a geography. You're ill-advised to tread on us, our self-respect, or our Social Security.

Above all, we Americans are an optimistic, democratic people. We will forgive just about everything from our politicians but condescension. Al Gore did worse than lie to us. He talked down to us.

He's not alone. The Democrats don't

have a monopoly on this crap. What about Dick Cheney cooking up energy policy in secret meetings with the oil boys? Locked doors, a bunch of policy wonks around the table, each pushing his agenda and ideology. Sounds like Hillary's recipe for health care. I don't like watching either party playing Father — or Mother — knows best.

This political assessment wasn't cultivated in a petri dish. It comes from thirty years that were roughly divided between working for politicians and covering them. Even as an insider I kept an outsider's attitude. When I wrote speeches for President Carter, my drinking buddies taunted me during the yearlong humiliation of the Iranian hostage crisis. When I worked as right-hand man for Tip O'Neill, I never forgot how much I had liked Ronald Reagan all those years on *GE Theater*. But before all that, I grew up in the America I talk and write about — in a family that, to use a discarded Clinton line, worked hard and played by the rules. Dad was intensely self-reliant. Mom was just as intensely suspicious of the country's cultural elite. My family background is as much a part of my political commentary as what I see in Washington.

It's what I know of this *real* America that fills these pages. The big fights today are not about economics — we pretty much agree on things like balanced budgets and free trade. It's not even about the usual laundry list of issues the politicians mentally — or literally — pull out of their pockets when asked what the next election is all about.

It's about this *attitude* of ours.

When you think about it, we Americans *are* different. That word "freedom" isn't just in our documents; it's in our cowboy souls. We are the most freedom-loving people in the world. We'd rather have guns than live under a government powerful enough to collect them all. We regularly say "no" to a British-style national health system, fearing it means a regime of long lines to see strange doctors. Many people with grave concerns about abortion would rather see women individually decide the matter rather than live under a government repressive enough to deny them the freedom to decide.

Nor are we Americans as cynical as some older cultures. After more than two hundred years of existence in a complex world, we continue to see life as a battle between the good guys and the bad guys. That's one reason Europeans love looking down on us.

Why can't we be more sophisticated, more worldly? Yet it is that very good guys versus bad guys mindset of ours that the same Europeans call upon when they face a real bad guy like Hitler or Stalin or Milosevic.

I know that mindset firsthand. My first job when I came to Washington three decades ago was as a .38-caliber-toting officer of the U.S. Capitol Police. It was in the old days when senators and members of Congress used the police jobs as patronage. Some of the slots went to sons of political pals so that these fortunate fellows could go to law school in D.C. My 3:00 to 11:00 p.m. shift was payback for working in a U.S. senator's office writing speeches and answering letters during the daytime.

But the core of the force was made up of lifers from the military, enlisted guys who'd done long hitches with the Army, Navy, or Marines.

I'd spend hours hanging out with these guys. My favorite was Sergeant Leroy Taylor. He was one of those citizen-philosophers who instinctively grasped this country's real politics, the kind that people live and are ready to die for. He and the other country boys would talk about how they would do anything to defend the Capitol. More than some of the big-shot elected officials, my colleagues in blue revered the place and what it meant to the republic. It wasn't about them, but about something much bigger.

I will never forget what Leroy once told me and the wisdom it contained: "The little man loves his country, Chris, because it's *all he's got.*"

I have never heard a better rendition of what I see as our unique American attitude. Or a sharper measure of the distance ordinary people feel from the economic and educated elites. Or a finer explanation of why, even with last year's then still-booming economy as his trump card, Al Gore isn't in the White House. Or why, when a real political gusher blows in this country, the establishment's finest always will be the last to yell. Or why, thank God, a guy with a partisan rap sheet like mine has earned the trust of so many conservatives, independents, and liberals as well who, like me, know just what Leroy Taylor was talking about.

George W. Bush

BE NOT AFRAID OF GREATNESS. SOME ARE
BORN GREAT, SOME ACHIEVE GREATNESS,
AND SOME HAVE GREATNESS THRUST UPON
THEM.

WILLIAM SHAKESPEARE

Few presidents are given the historic duty to lead America through a crisis like the World Trade Center horror. Not since Vietnam had the country felt so violated. Not since World War II had we felt such resolve. We wanted orders and we looked to one man to give them.

In the days following September 11, 2001, George W. Bush displayed a presidential *command* that warmed his supporters and impressed even his nastiest critics. Championing America's ardor, he launched a global campaign against terrorism.

"Tonight we are a country awakened to danger and called to defend freedom," he told the Congress and the country. "Our grief has turned to anger, and anger to resolution. Whether we bring our enemies to justice or bring justice to our enemies, justice will be done."

In Bush, the country discovered it had a young leader rising to the occasion, an easygoing Prince Hal transformed by instinct and circumstance into a warrior King Henry. A president who once suffered daily questions about his legitimacy now commanded the backing of nine in ten Americans. No president in modern time had captured such overwhelming loyalty in a matter of such historic peril.

It was not the first time Bush displayed an unexpected audacity. In 1994, he took on Texas governor Ann Richards when she was a national icon, and beat her. When he saw the TV networks prematurely calling Florida for Al Gore in 2000, he invited the national cameras into the family hotel suite. There, in the presence of the former president and first lady, parents George and Barbara, he scolded the press into backing down. "The people actually counting the votes have come to a different perspective," he told the country, especially those supporters in the western states still heading to the polls. "I'm pretty darn upbeat about things."

Had events gone a little differently that

night, George W. Bush could have been *barbecued* by the media for hiding behind Daddy and Mommy. It was such a personal call on his part that I credit him with bold leadership. With that single risky performance he changed the election night's dynamic. Instead of being seen as a loser the morning after and throughout the five weeks of recounts and legal arguments, the man hunkered down on his Texas farm seemed to most Americans like the winner.

So we knew Bush had nerve. What we wondered about was how much depth there was to the guy. Was he more cerebral than he seemed? Was he a sneaky "grind" who went off and studied things when nobody was looking? Did he possess some special instinct for leadership, some unexplained knack for calling the shots under pressure?

Like so many others, I carried this conflicted view of George W. Bush right into the World Trade Center and Pentagon crisis. Remember what I said after that third presidential debate with Al Gore? I said Bush was "not prepared to be president in many ways." I still think that was a fair assessment. There were things this son of a president didn't know, didn't have the curiosity to learn. At times it seemed that others, led by Vice President Cheney, were calling the shots.

One reason for this perception may be Bush's executive style. As a manager, he follows the "hidden hand" pattern of President Eisenhower. Like Ike, he has filled his cabinet with CEOs and governors. Like Ike, he *invested* in each cabinet member. Look at the way Bush handled the Chinese government's retention of the downed EP3 reconnaissance plane. He left it to Colin Powell to use the language and cultural expertise of the State Department to find the right words to appease Beijing. Then, once the crewmen were home, he let Defense Secretary Don Rumsfeld defend the honor, performance, and morale of the military by telling the world that our guys were right, the Chinese fighter pilot was wrong.

But for many months in 2001 the new presidency seemed to stall. With an entire country ready to know and like him, Bush clung to familiar company, familiar geography, familiar thinking. He acted as if the only Republicans were southern Republicans. Why did he spend so much time down on his Texas ranch when he could have been forging new alliances that could give him a clear majority in 2004? "I'm amongst friends in Texas," he said, in explaining his month-long trip home in August 2001. But couldn't he have been *making* friends up in places like the Philly suburbs, near where I grew up?

I have to admit that during that August vacation in Texas, Bush managed to pull a head-fake on the American press corps. Under the cover of a four-week vacation, he delivered a prime-time speech on stem cell research that won a 70 percent approval rating. Even more successful were his Jimmy Carter-like house building with Habitat for Humanity and his Ronald Reagan-like brush clearing in the Rockies. Those who denigrate such vivid imagery as "form over function" ignore how this Yale-educated cowboy got his job.

I noticed something else about George W. He was operating at a 180 degree angle from his father. The forty-first president raised taxes; the forty-third couldn't wait to lower them. Forty-one emphasized foreign policy; forty-three began his presidency with a narrow focus on the home front. The father kept remote from the religious right. The son has kept this particular alliance fresh.

HERE'S WHAT I REALLY THINK: Every time you lower the bar on this fellow, the easier it becomes for him to clear it.

When he spoke to the nation about stem

cells, for example, President George W. Bush admitted right up front that such issues are not solvable by brainpower alone. Good people disagree on the subject. Nobody's necessarily right, nobody's necessarily been proven wrong. We're all in this together, trying to square our religious views with our medical hopes, our deepest human values with our scientific potential.

Before the World Trade Center and Pentagon tragedies, however, Bush had failed to project a clear sense of national purpose. There was no music to his presidency. I'm talking about that optimistic cadence that has lifted the nation in the past. I'm talking about an American *mission*.

On September 11, 2001, that mission was thrust upon him. Through instinct and compassion, he stood in the rubble of the World Trade Center and forged an almost sacramental bond with the American people. Surrounded by New York firemen, he seemed exactly where he belonged.

"I will not forget this wound to our country, or those who inflicted it," he told the country later. "I will not yield. I will not rest. I will not relent in waging this struggle for the freedom and security of the American people." As no president before he united the American people on a course of both purpose and peril.

Whether success for the country and greatness for the president will follow depends on history not yet written.

Chapter Two

The Man with the Sun

in His Face

ALL MEN DREAM; BUT NOT EQUALLY.
THOSE WHO DREAM BY NIGHT IN THE
DUSTY RECESSES OF THEIR MINDS WAKE IN
THE DAY TO FIND THAT IT WAS VANITY;
BUT THE DREAMERS OF THE DAY ARE DAN-
GEROUS MEN, FOR THEY MAY ACT THEIR
DREAM WITH OPEN EYES, TO MAKE IT POS-
SIBLE. THIS I DID.

T. E. LAWRENCE,
Seven Pillars of Wisdom

Professors of political *science* — talk about an oxymoron! — like to construct elaborate formulae to predict our elections. You can tell how many previous models failed by the number of variables required in the latest.

My model has just one variable: Look for the candidate you picture with the sun in his face.

I present to you a slide show:

FDR arriving in his open roadster to visit the troops

Harry Truman giving 'em hell from the back of a train

Ike riding down the canyons of Wall Street, the ticker tape streaming down from the high-floored windows, his hands raised up with the V-sign, his smile as wide as Kansas

JFK looking like a million bucks, hand-combing his hair off his forehead, a crowd of "jumpers" straining to get a look at his gleaming teeth, his Palm Beach–tanned face

Ronald Reagan standing on the bluffs of Normandy paying grand tribute to the boys of Point de Hoc or clearing brush in cowboy denim at his Rancho del Cielo

These are the hero presidents. We think of them with the full flush of the outdoors shining on their cheeks.

And the losers: Tom Dewey, Adlai Stevenson, Mike Dukakis, Al Gore. We think of them, when we think of them at all, as men in blue suits behind desks.

Sometimes, as in the 1968 face-off between Dick Nixon and Hubert Humphrey, the sun is nowhere to be found. Sometimes we pick a windswept winner only to see him degenerate into a desk jockey. A confident, sunburned farmer in '76, Jimmy Carter became a workaholic prisoner of the Rose Garden. A man running as Ronald Reagan's third term, George Herbert Walker Bush, became instead a D.C.-based backroom banker.

In modern elections we get the chance to see and hear what a candidate is really *like*, and this intimate scrutiny makes voting an increasingly personal decision. We root for the guy running against the "suits," the guy we can imagine suitless himself.

Think, if you can, of Bill Clinton the first time we met him, the gung-ho boomer leaping full-grown from the heartland into our consciousness. Think of George W. Bush who, despite his patrician origins and Yale degree, ran successfully as a Texas cowboy against the bland and bookish Gore. Although we Americans may vote indoors, we seem to want to elect presidents with the look, feel, and freshness of America the beautiful. It connects with our blue-skies optimism, perhaps even to something deep in our national myth.

HERE'S WHAT I REALLY THINK: Want to

pick the winner next time? Find the *man with the sun in his face.* If Bush gets driven indoors, is forced to defend his job by posing in the Oval Office, bet on the other guy. If he retains his outside-the-Beltway persona, bet on the incumbent.

When friends come to Washington these days, I take them, often late at night, to visit the new Franklin Roosevelt monument on the Tidal Basin. I take them there, but I don't really like it. It must be the moonlit geography that invites me back. It's definitely not the message. Whoever built this memorial decided somehow that it would be a great idea to commemorate the grimness of the Great Depression. There are statues of mournful men waiting in breadlines. There's FDR sitting in his wheelchair, images not of what Roosevelt achieved but of what he was up against.

I hate it, and I'm sure the great man himself would have hated it. It would be like naming an IRS building after Ronald Reagan. Why didn't the FDR Memorial planners go all the way and add to the site depictions of Japanese Zeroes dropping bombs on Pearl Harbor or Hitler marching through Poland?

Now, HERE'S WHAT I REALLY THINK:

Want to see a real monument to Franklin Roosevelt? It's the Social Security system that he insisted be financed by workers and employers alike. It's the free enterprise system he saved by that "bold and timely experimentation" of his, otherwise known as the New Deal.

If FDR had been as downbeat as this morbid memorial — a project, I might add, that he asked not be undertaken anyhow — he never would have been elected in the first place. We vote our dreams when we elect presidents, not our nightmares. If you don't get that about we Americans you don't get us. To save the "forgotten man" in 1932 we chose a winner, a fellow riding in an open roadster, his cigarette holder jutting skyward at a neat forty-five degrees.

"Meeting Franklin Roosevelt," his war ally Winston Churchill once wrote, "was like having your first glass of champagne." "A man with a third-class mind but a first-class *temperament*," said John Maynard Keynes.

It was that upbeat temperament of his that made all the difference both at home and in war. Columnist Joseph Alsop wrote of being in Hong Kong the day after Pearl Harbor and listening, as the Japanese bombs fell, to Roosevelt address Congress:

The radio was so faulty that I had to lie on the floor with my head just under it in order to hear much of anything. I got the president's drift, which was easy enough to predict in any case, but I caught no more than one word in two — hardly more than enough to be reminded of the timbre of his voice. Yet in these fairly gloomy and frustrating circumstances, it never for one moment occurred to me that there might be the smallest doubt about the outcome of the vast war the president was asking the Congress to declare. Nor did I find any other American throughout the entire war who ever doubted the eventual outcome. Even more than the feeling that there were giants in the land, I now feel nostalgia for the absolute confidence in the American future, which was the necessary foundation of this total absence of doubt. Hope was in fact Franklin Roosevelt's greatest gift to his fellow Americans.

AL GORE

He reminds me of something Jack Kennedy once told a British journalist about Richard Nixon: "Nixon is a nice fellow in private, and a very able man. I worked with him on the Hill for a long time, but it seems he has a split personality and he is very bad in public."

Both are true of Al Gore. In person, he has a good sense of humor, is capable of enjoying the moment. On Air Force Two he could be a warm host. At a Georgetown party, he can be an easy fellow guest. He can also be stone-faced, profoundly aristocratic. He can use his position to intimidate the other person. I've seen him in all these personas.

In public, Gore can simply seem robotic. I once watched him address a large international group of Green party politicians in the Capitol. Instead of a warm welcome, he used his after-dinner remarks to read a printed address. It was as if he'd arrived in a Federal Express envelope.

It's really a problem of multiple public personalities. Again, there's the Nixon parallel. Jack Kennedy once told an ally that he felt sorry for Nixon because he did not know who he was, and at each stop he had to decide which Nixon he was at the moment, which had to have been very exhausting.

In the three presidential debates of 2000, Vice-President Gore showed the country three different Alberts. First came the over-bearing know-it-all. Then came the reces-sive, passive guy. Finally, there arrived the hybrid, the self Gore promoted in his postdebate spin session as "just right."

The public, perhaps dizzy from too much time tracking Gore through the funhouse mirror of his campaign, didn't agree. They knew Goldilocks. They grew up with Goldilocks. Al Gore was no Goldilocks. If he reminded us of any figure from our col-lective youths it was the movie-star-turned-TV-hostess Loretta Young, known for wearing a new dress for every scene.

Then there's the Clinton problem. When he knew Clinton was lying publicly about Monica, and he must have known almost immediately, he should have made a simple, indelible statement along the lines that "a president should not lie to the American people." Clinton wouldn't have liked it, and the party hacks would have muttered bad things about the importance of "dancing with the one that brung you," but Al Gore would have stood out at a critical time as a leader with a sense of honor. He would have marked himself, and been marked by the country, as his own man. The country would have known it had at least one national officeholder with a hard and fast commitment to preserving the honor of his high office.

Instead Gore offered himself as a character out of *The Last Hurrah*, a Ditto Boland repeating "the governah's" words as if gospel. Looking for a future leader, a replacement to the dishonored Clinton, the voters couldn't spot one, not until George W. Bush came along offering to respect not just the Constitution but also something Gore could not dare mention for the tragic reason that he had failed to when it mattered: the honor of the office.

Gore spent too much of the 2000 election itself going on the negative. He even manufactured a claim that his dog paid a cheaper price than his mother-in-law for the same arthritis medicine. That set the tone. Having spent his entire life preparing for the presidency, he spent the summer and fall trying to *scare* people into voting for him. It was not a pretty picture. He had the strongest asset an incumbent can carry into an election: *It's the economy, stupid!* But he blew it.

Al Gore should have said, when it mattered most, that it is important that an American president not tell lies to the people. He didn't. Instead he led the cheers for Clinton on the day the House of Representatives voted the articles of impeachment. How much better it would have been for him and the country had the vice-president made himself plain that day, had he said what he was thinking: Bill Clinton's indictment by the Congress was *Bill Clinton's* fault.

Instead, Gore called Clinton "a man I believe will be regarded in the history books as one of our greatest presidents." He watched the galloping horse of history ride through the Rose Garden, but could not or would not pull himself up into the saddle.

Even as a Faustian deal it made no sense. Why would Gore, who did not deserve an iota of blame for the Monica Lewinsky affair itself, sell his soul to Clinton in 1998, only to then welsh on the deal two years later? Why would he kneel before the master at the moment when the master's words were dishonest, his actions contemptible? Why would he then break so unceremoniously from Clinton in 2000? When it came time to share the bragging rights for the strong economy, Gore acted like he'd never met the man.

I repeat: If Gore had made a one-sentence statement in 1998 — "A president should not lie to the American people" — I believe he would be president today. Yes, he would have angered Clinton. Clinton would have stayed angry for anywhere from ten days to two weeks. Then, liberated from his sycophancy, Gore could have invited his boss to join him in a 2000 victory lap.

By his timidity, which he undoubtedly told himself was loyalty, Al Gore ended up looking to voters like the Clinton era's bathtub ring. Americans want more of their leaders than that.

There is nothing final in my assessment of Al Gore, and I think he will one day build for himself a more defensible legacy. I cite as Exhibit A his stunning concession speech. It was clearly the finest thing said by anyone in recent American history. What distinguished it was its target audience. For the first time in the campaign, perhaps in his life, Gore rejected the kind of ethnic and pressure group pandering that had been his trademark. He spoke instead to the American people as a whole. In the wake of the five-to-four Supreme Court ruling that stopped the hand recounts in Florida, his message was unity, not division.

"Not under man but under God and law," he said.

> That's the ruling principle of American freedom, the source of our democratic liberties. I tried to make it my guide throughout this contest as it has guided America's deliberations of all the complex issues of the past five weeks. Now the U.S. Supreme Court has spoken. Let there be no doubt, while I strongly disagree with the Court's decision, I accept it. I accept the finality of this outcome, which will be ratified next Monday in the Electoral College. And tonight, for the sake of our unity of the people and the strength of our democracy, I offer my concession.

Gore's words carried a sound and sense similar to perhaps the greatest American speech ever, Lincoln's second inaugural address. Referring to the Civil War, Lincoln said, "Both parties deprecated war, but one of them would make war rather than let the country survive, and the other would accept war rather than let it perish. Then the war came." Gore offered some of the same fatalism speaking of his own loss to Bush: "Neither he nor I anticipated this long and difficult road. Certainly neither of us wanted it to happen. Yet, it came, and now has ended, resolved, as it must be resolved, through the honored institutions of our democracy."

Having risen through the country's civil institutions — the House, the Senate, the vice-presidency — Gore was renewing his oath to support them. I'll say it again: It is the best thing Al Gore has ever said, the best thing anyone has said in this contentious society for a long, long while. What would have happened had he discovered the same strength and honor during the Clinton mess? Who knows what *will* happen if Gore returns to the political arena speaking with as much nobility and selflessness as he did when he left.

I predict that when Al Gore runs again for president, and he certainly will, he is destined to command a slew of potent advantages:

1. In 2000, he won more votes than any Democrat in history, with fifty-one million votes to Clinton's forty-seven million in 1996.

2. His victory in the popular vote gives him a tremendous claim on his party for another chance to win in the Electoral College.

3. The most diehard Democrats, and this includes many African-American voters, would love to see the man they think was robbed last time take it away from Bush the next time.

4. Gore will be the only Democrat in the field with the experience of having run a general election campaign for president.

5. Gore knows, better than anyone on earth, which states he lost that he could win next time with a new, improved strategy. Put Tennessee at the top of the list.

HERE'S WHAT I REALLY THINK: In the end, Al Gore will run for president again because it is the one, the *only,* thing he wants to do in life. He has not just the strong desire to run for president, but also, somewhere down deep in him, the necessary reverence for the office itself. If there's one thing worse than spending the rest of his life thinking and rethinking how he could have won in 2000, it's spending the rest of his life knowing that he failed to try again. Even if he runs and loses, he will leave the stage as a gutsy warrior. Moreover, Eugene

McCarthy, as the perennial candidate himself, once told me, "It's easier to run for president than to *stop*."

CHAPTER THREE

GOD AND COUNTRY

I DECLINE UTTERLY TO BE IMPARTIAL BE-
TWEEN THE FIRE BRIGADE AND THE FIRE.
WINSTON CHURCHILL

When people ask me how long it takes to prepare for *Hardball* each day, I recite my regular regimen. Kathy and I get up, we see the
kids off to school, read *The Washington Post*
and *The New York Times*, then I have my regular 8:45 phone chat with executive producer
Phil Griffin. I could go on like this, re-
counting my daily routine, but if you want
the honest answer to how much time it takes
to prepare for *Hardball*, it's half a century.

I know that because, while I can't always
whip off the list of guests I had on *Hardball*
last night, I can remember certain things
that happened to me fifty years ago. One
was a dream I had. It was in Cinemascope. I
was leading a cavalry charge across the
plains of Russia, leading America to victory
over the Communist enemy.

My other memory is of an argument I had with my first-grade teacher.

"Master Matthews!"

There were one hundred kids in our class at the Maternity of the Blessed Virgin Mary school in Philadelphia, and Sister Mildred was looking unmistakably at the kid sitting in the far-left corner of the back row — *me.* Her long wooden pointer just as unmistakably tapped at a two-letter word she had chalked on the blackboard.

"U. . . . S.," I said, as sure of myself as I would ever be again.

"Those are the letters," she said, her patience well in check. "What do they spell?"

"U. . . . S.," I repeated, assuming she just wanted to make sure the class heard me giving the correct answer.

"Yes," she kept on. "But what does it *spell?*" At this point Sister had lost her patience.

What is her problem? I thought to myself, as the situation tensed.

As clear as that standoff at Maternity BVM is to me today, I forget just how it ended. Still, I'm positive it was a preview of things to come. I saw the world one way. She saw it another. To Sister Mildred the two letters "u" and "s" meant first person plural. To me, it spelled the "U.S." It meant

America. "U.S." was the word newspapers used in the war headlines, the insignia our fighting men wore on their uniforms. Sister Mildred was talking about some mundane pronoun. I was thinking about my country.

Such evidence, admittedly anecdotal, suggests I was operating on a different level from other kids in grade school. I always wondered, to be perfectly truthful, why I was so much more aware of America's position in the world than they were. I wasn't odd. *They* were.

One person I have to credit for this precocious worldliness is my older brother Bert. Even before first grade, Bert and I had fought countless skirmishes in the vast "outback" of our new house on the rural Philadelphia border of Bucks County. Against the backdrop of vacant farmhouses, I would take the role of the Germans and Bert the "U.S.," or American, side. The next day we'd switch and I would be the "U.S." and he'd play the "Japanese."

When the Korean War broke out in 1950, Bert would be the American side and I'd be the "Commies." We were happy once again to have a war going on. It made not just our games but somehow life itself grander. Even at that young age, I knew that this was America, that we were the good guys, and that we had never lost a war.

Boomers like me who attended Catholic school back in the years just after World War II remember how patriotic we were. That Pledge of Allegiance we recited was just a token of the devotion we showed our country. Just as they would honor every "feast day" on the liturgical calendar, the nuns always seemed to be leading us in parades up and down Bustleton Avenue to celebrate one national holiday or another.

By third grade, the threat of a new and more horrible war had come closer to home. The Communists now had both the A-bomb and the H-bomb. If war came, both sides would be using them, and there would be no winner.

In those days we had two types of safety drills in school. The fire drill was when we marched in line out of the classroom and into the recess yard. The air raid drill was when we crouched under our little wooden desks. We would then wait for fifteen minutes, smelling the varnish and imagining the predicted "flash of light" — the world's end, and the general judgment — when all the human beings who ever lived would stand before God and be judged for their sins. (Honesty was a very important lesson to learn as a kid — especially when paired with the idea that at any moment you could die and be held accountable for any deceit, small or large, in your life.)

Even back then this was all great material for black humor. I used to imagine how funny it would be if they got the two drill bells mixed up. How we'd be crouching under our balsa wooden desks when the fire came or how we'd be out on the "blacktop" to greet the incoming ICBMs.

I'm sure all the crouching and counting the minutes until the promised "flash" had to have had an effect on us. The early Cold War, with its rich specter of nuclear cataclysm, added to the schizoid quality of what would be known currently as our "early childhood development." I'm sure the nuns loved the chance to incorporate their entire worldview into that single ritual of hiding under our desks from the atomic raid. Here was America and Russia, good and evil, life and death, sin and punishment, all wrapped up into a perfectly synchronized quarter hour.

This rehearsing for doomsday affected we boomers just as the Depression had shaped the generation before. I remember telling a kindly aunt with great pride that I'd just been hired to work for the Carter White House.

"Is that a permanent job?" she asked.

Her response was the result of having grown up too close to the unemployment lines. American childhoods of the early Cold War produced, I think, a different instinct. While my father's generation might regard the basement as a place to *hide* a jar of quarters in case those breadlines started forming again, those of us faced at an early age with the prospect of falling A-bombs think of the basement as a place to hide.

The live specter of the apocalypse *now* also encourages short-term thinking. If people my age are awkward about financial planning, it may well be because, as teens and young adults in the 1960s, we never scheduled beyond Saturday night. The reason people like me are so focused on patriotism and morality and the big picture is that we were drilled early to confront the prospect of life on earth ending in a flash and something far more daunting arriving instantly in its place. Martyrdom, and the more grizzly the better, was the central story line in 1950s Catholicism. We repeatedly heard lurid accounts of those who had died for their faiths. The most unforgettable, as told by the Sisters of Mercy, was that of the biblical "Seven Brothers" in the book of the Maccabees. It began when one brother told the king that he, his siblings, and their mother would rather die than eat the forbidden pork. Enraged, the king ordered the stubborn youth's tongue, hands, and feet cut off. After that had been done, his mother and brothers were forced to throw him onto a boiling vat of oil. This process was then repeated for each member of the family. Thanks to the good Sisters, the fact that they all died for their faith was seared into us.

I remember the day in the spring of 1953 that Stalin died. I remember that Sister instructed us all to offer up some prayers. I remember wondering what exactly we were praying for? That the Soviet dictator get a surefire send-off to you know where? That God would forgive him? That he might undergo a death-bed conversion to Catholicism like the Jewish gangster Dutch Schultz? Or had the nuns simply gone on automatic pilot, getting us all to pray simply because something really important was happening?

HERE'S WHAT I REALLY THINK: I think that growing up where and when I did explains my instinctive on-air connection between God and country, morality and politics. It's a good guy–bad guy game in which the good guys are forever endangered.

I admire a great line my friend Peggy Noonan wrote for the first president Bush: "America is not just another pleasant country in the UN roll call somewhere between Albania and Zimbabwe."

Like Peggy, I believe in American exceptionalism. We were raised to believe in it, raised to believe that when Kate Smith sang "God Bless America" she was singing *our* song, raised to believe that the prayer we said at the end of each Sunday mass for the "conversion of Russia" someday would be heard.

I know that none of this is politically correct today. We're supposed to think multilaterally, to think of ways we can behave like other countries and stop thinking of what makes us different. We're not even supposed to call ourselves "Americans." How chauvinist! Don't we realize how that rankles the Canadians and the Mexicans and all the others who share this hemisphere north and south? How dare we engage in triumphalism?

This is the country that sold the world on democracy, on free markets, and, increasingly, on human rights. We should be doing victory laps.

I say this because, for my generation, the Communist threat did not die with Stalin.

There were times when it looked very much like we would either lose the Cold War or perish in some horrid, all-out nuclear war begun by accident, or by what Jack Kennedy called a "miscalculation."

In 1956 we watched the gutsy Hungarians lob cobblestones at the Soviet tanks and could do nothing to help them. In 1957, we saw the Soviets launch *Sputnik* despite regular assurances from Walt Disney and his pal Werner Von Braun that America would be the first to put a satellite into space. We watched the red on the world map spread from Asia to Africa to South America, even to our doorstep. We suffered the historic tragedy of Vietnam trying to stop it. As recently as the late seventies, we watched the Soviets overrun Afghanistan and place brigades in Cuba. As late as the eighties, polls showed that many Americans still worried about a nuclear war with the slowly advancing Communists. And then, thank God, everything changed.

Why then am I so unforgiving toward the hard left? Because they spent most of the Cold War saying that Communism was simply an alternative economic system. I'm so hard on the *anti*-anti-Communists because I don't quite *get* them. Why would anyone have a problem with resisting what was a real threat to this country? Even when I thought Vietnam had become a horrible mistake, I never understood those who cheered for Ho Chi Minh. It's the same reason I am slow to accept Fidel Castro as a trading partner. Had the Cold War gone the other way, he would have been in the reviewing stand for the executions. He would have relished the moment, just as he took delight in sending his sadistic intelligence officers to torture American POWs in Hanoi.

Why do I still hate the Communists? Because we could have lost it all to them. Why do I have a problem with Bill Clinton? Because this child of the early boomer generation seems to have grown up with absolutely none of its legacy, none of the history and anti-Communist fervor, and none of the awe for the presidency he found so easy both to win and to abuse.

BILL CLINTON

I have no idea who William Jefferson Clinton is. When he was first elected governor of Arkansas, my impression was of an Ivy League–taught southerner whom the sixties had carried happily leftward. Defeated for reelection, he made his Little Rock comeback as a capital-punishing good ol' boy. Then when he ran for president in 1991, he offered himself as a Democratic Leadership Council conservative, blasting "quotas" and other evils of the liberal establishment. But that's when he expected to face New York governor Mario Cuomo. When Cuomo failed to join the race, Clinton headed left again, savaging poor Paul Tsongas when he tried taking the centrist position that he, Bill Clinton, had just deserted.

Elected president, Clinton pushed the old-time religion of boondoggle spending — a "stimulus package," he called it — and a big-government answer to the country's health care challenge. Losing control of Congress in 1994, he switched again, declaring the era of big government over, and signed a Republican-written welfare reform bill.

I'd like to be able to say this ideological fickleness didn't fool me, but I can't.

My first in-person contact with the man came in 1991, when I covered the Democratic Leadership Council's annual meeting in Cleveland. Governor Clinton gave the major address, and he was a colossal success. In his speech he railed against deadbeat dads, demanding that they be brought to justice and forced to pay for their children's upbringing. He assaulted "quotas" and generally pushed all the right buttons for a crowd largely made up of corporate and trade association conservatives seeking an opportunity to gain influence in the Democratic party. He played the crowd like a banjo. On the way home, I wrote a column saying the conservative Democrats had found their hero.

But what I was witnessing in Cleveland was not so much an illumination of Bill Clinton's gut philosophy as it was an exhibition of his astounding skill at political *positioning*. Expecting Mario Cuomo to run for the presidential nomination the following year, he figured his opportunities were in the center and right rather than in the left. Once Cuomo withdrew, it created an opening in the Democratic mainstream, at which point Bill Clinton abruptly abandoned his conservative rhetoric. The revised strategy was to let poor ex-senator Paul Tsongas carry the banner for Social Security and Medicare reform. Clinton would spend the rest of the nomination fight tearing apart Tsongas's efforts to adjust the Democratic party to the reality that the programs they had created were in bad need of repair. Clinton pandered to the party's hope for deliverance from these cruel choices, leaving Tsongas the thankless task of telling the truth.

In the New Hampshire primary Bill Clinton would, of course, suffer through a more personal confession. When old flame Gennifer Flowers held a press conference, Bill and Hillary were forced onto *60 Minutes* to defend their marriage in front of the entire universe. But the affair with Gennifer never hurt. It was old, she was a grown-up, and its connection to official business was, at best, tenuous.

Clinton's problem was his lack of candor in dealing with the tempest Flowers had raised. He denied, for example, that it was his voice on a tape she played at her press conference. Then, ignoring the denial, Clinton apologized for something said on it, an ethnic slur the voice on the tape had un-leashed at Governor Cuomo.

An even more bogus denial, if we can cali-brate Clinton's work in this way, dealt with the draft notice the Arkansas governor had gotten as a young man. Clinton told the press that he couldn't remember getting it. It's safe to say that no one of our generation exposed to the military draft of the 1960s can *imagine* forgetting such an event. Yet that's what Clinton claimed in the cam-paign, that he did not remember being drafted. That was the first clear indication of his chronic problem with the truth. Not only was it a flagrant lie, his arrogant insis-tence on the obvious untruth suggested an in-your-face feudalism: *I am your master, you are the serf. I can lie to you and you have to take it.*

I remember being in a mob of reporters in an airport hangar the Wednesday before the New Hampshire primary. Clinton flack-catchers James Carville and Frank Greer were wandering around in their usual spin cycle, claiming that a 1969 letter from Clinton thanking the head of the ROTC at the University of Arkansas for "saving" him from the draft wasn't what it appeared. From what I could see, Clinton had played a number on this ROTC commander, talking him into granting a draft deferment based on a promise to join the ROTC. It's just that young Bill never did. For him, the ROTC was a fallback position he never had to assume. To me this was yet another example of his reflexive dishonesty.

It was all hard evidence that Bill Clinton had discovered at a very young age that you can get away with making commitments and reneging on them once the situation changes. Intuitively he grasped the unwritten statute of limitations on indignation. People simply can't stay focused forever on someone else's alibi.

I remember the morning after the New Hampshire primary, Clinton had gone up on the stage at his headquarters after the polls closed the night before to crown himself the "Comeback Kid." Paul Tsongas had won by eight percentage points, but somehow he let Clinton steal the night from him. It was an amazingly orchestrated charade.

Clinton walked into the *Good Morning America* studio that a.m. like a winner, surrounded by a phalanx of blue suits. He went directly for the doughnuts. A few minutes after he left, a sheepish guy arrived wearing a schoolkid's book bag over his shoulder. With a lone staffer at his side, Paul Tsongas said, "Do you think I could have one of those doughnuts over there on the table?" He didn't stand a chance.

The underlying truth to Bill Clinton's role as the Comeback Kid is that he constantly needed to come back. He was always in the process of falling down and picking himself back up again. His return to the Arkansas governor's chair in 1982 was a comeback victory after being bounced from it in 1980. His second-place finish in the New Hampshire primary was a "comeback" only because he had blown an earlier lead. The public would never quite get used to the fact that his dance was always a two-step, and that this self-crowned Comeback Kid would be forever creating the need for a comeback. It was all part of a cycle of alternating arrogance and apology.

I say all this as someone who found himself early in 1991 falling for the Clinton pitch. He promised early on to battle for those "who work hard and play by the rules," a surefire connection with someone like me. As he had with millions of others, Clinton had found the combination to my political safe. He also said he wanted to make abortion "safe, legal, and rare." That was another shrewdly crafted appeal to people of my bent.

The great tragedy of Bill Clinton is that so many of us wanted to trust him. And one of the great disappointments of the Clinton-Monica fandango was the desperate need for one Democratic leader, one member of his cabinet, one member of his staff to come forward and say, "I will not participate in this cover-up. I will not be a party to a president's use of his official position to promulgate a lie to the American people."

No one did.

Another point: Bill Clinton was less popular among men, more popular among women. That's a switch from his purported role model, Jack Kennedy. Kennedy made men, especially those his age, feel like they were part of the action. Like many of them, he had been a junior officer in World War II. His rise to commander-in-chief was their triumph too. Clinton, on the other hand, hoarded the prize. I do not understand why a man like Bill Clinton, blessed as he is with extraordinary political skills, did not use those same political skills to become not just president, but a great president. Instead, he contented himself with a reign as the country's prom king.

What it comes down to, I've come to think, is a lack of *reverence*. A man who shows so little respect for his historic circumstances could not find a way to win historic respect. I just don't *get* how a man who could get the hard part couldn't get the easy part.

CHAPTER FOUR

PEOPLE WHO WORK HARD

AND PLAY BY THE RULES

THE UPPER CLASSES ARE A NATION'S PAST;
THE MIDDLE CLASS IS ITS FUTURE.

AYN RAND

Anyone who reflects honestly realizes that we inherit our family politics the same way we do the family religion. We may not vote like our moms and dads, but we find ourselves, often against our will, feeling and even talking like them.

One afternoon in a downtown Philadelphia movie theater, a five-star general with a big smile appeared in the newsreel. I can't remember exactly — I was six at the time — but I have a picture in my mind of him boarding a plane from one of those old portable airplane stairs.

"Is he president?" I asked Dad, who was sitting in the seat just to my right.

"No," he answered with calm assurance, "but he *will* be!"

The year was 1952, and our family definitely liked "Ike" — Dwight D. Eisenhower, the military leader who had just seven years before accepted the documents of Nazi surrender.

That fall, riding the bus to school, I staked out my position publicly. I was for Eisenhower. The lonely voice of opposition was that of my second-grade classmate Mike Matthews — no relation — whose father was the local Democratic committeeman. Practically everyone else I knew either liked Ike or kept his opinion to himself.

So now you know my ideological parentage. Dad, for purposes of classification, was a practical conservative, the kind of Republican you find in the Northeast, say, in Pennsylvania and New Jersey. When I asked Dad who would win in a boxing match, Kennedy or Nixon, he didn't let his politics harm his handicapping. "Kennedy would kill him," he said, with not a second's hesitation.

While Dad sympathized with the Communist hunters, he thought Senator Joseph McCarthy "went too far." When I fell for Goldwater in the early sixties — don't forget, Hillary Rodham did too — Dad questioned the Arizona senator's plan to make Social Security voluntary. He predicted that people would opt out of the system when they were making money, and then end up on welfare when they stopped. A profoundly self-reliant figure, Dad approved of government programs of the self-help variety. He went through college after World War II on the GI bill. He put us through first-rate colleges thanks to those National Defense Education Act loans triggered into existence by the *Sputnik* scare.

My father was the hardest worker I have ever known. Whenever I have to work late at night and feel like quitting, I think about how dedicated he was, and how uncompromising. For thirty years he was an official reporter in the Philadelphia County court system. During the mornings and well into the afternoon, he would record hours of court testimony. Then he would come home on the train and work until ten o'clock dictating his notes into a dictaphone, breaking only for dinner.

I think Dad got his worker-bee genes from his mother. Grandmom-in-Chestnut-Hill, as we called her, was also a provider. An immigrant from Northern Ireland in her teens, widowed in her fifties, she built a one-person laundry service, serving the network of wealthy families she and Grandpop, born in England, had long worked for. Wildly beloved by all who knew her, she spoke with an Irish accent and conveyed a strong, upbeat, fun-loving attitude her entire life. She not only supported herself but made sure there was always a regular flow of gifts to her grandchildren. For birthdays and Christmas I could count on getting the latest historical biography from the Frigate Bookstore in Chestnut Hill.

While Dad kept a roof over our heads, Mom instilled in us our ambition and direction. Here is what I wrote about Mom in September 1996. It's also, as you'll see, about Dad.

"I have a picture of my mom, who died last week, from that grand trip we took to Washington in 1954. She's standing with her three elder boys at this country's one, true national shrine, the Lincoln Memorial.

The picture tells quite a story, not just of four sunny days in Washington, but of my mother's aspirations for her five sons.

It is, I can see now, a very American story.

Mary Shields grew up in a North Philadelphia rowhouse at a time and a place where people — they were mostly Irish Catholic — knew each other by their parish. Mom's marriage to Dad, a Protestant, constituted her first major break from this world.

My mother had ambitions, most of all for her sons. When Dad got out of the Navy at the end of World War II, she encouraged him to get his bachelor's degree under the GI Bill.

She and he made the even bigger jump of moving from the old church-dominated neighborhood to an area of converted farmland near Bucks County my grandparents would forever view as 'God's country.'

The move was symbolic of wider aspirations that would reveal themselves in the years to follow.

Mom had dreams for us. They began with piano lessons. We were to be children of talent. Next came braces for our teeth. Then came private school. All five of us would attend one of the finest in the city. And college. I had my choice of Georgetown, Notre Dame and Holy Cross.

These totems of privilege were achieved as much through sacrifice as dollars-and-cents income. It was not the size of Dad's paycheck but the way both my parents decided to spend it.

I never knew anyone to work as long or as hard as my father, nor anyone to dream so highly for her children as my mother. My middle-income parents somehow managed to raise their children as upper-middle-income.

My mother had known a far different childhood. College had been out of the question. The minute she graduated from high school she was made to work and pay 'board,' turning over each pay envelope to her Depression-weary mother. Just as her mother ruled the pocketbook, her strict father ruled the house.

The greatest restriction was on what she could do with her life. Ambition, like college, was not discussed. She was expected to live just as she was raised herself.

Mom had other ideas. Just as she hoped, her greatest gift to us, her most loving legacy, was that most American of all notions: that the way things are is not necessarily the way they are going to be.

People, given the will, can choose lives much different from those of their parents.

I will never forget the excuse letter Mom wrote my third-grade teacher to explain that '54 trip to Washington. She said that my father was taking us for 'business' reasons. My parents' real business in Washington was exposing their three older boys to their country's capital.

The trip was unforgettable. I remember the shaded slave quarters at Mount Vernon, endless rows of ancient bicycles at the Smithsonian, the elevator to the top of the Washington Monument, the trips to those other great memorials on the Mall.

I came back from that trip with a fateful souvenir: an enduring, vivid notion of 'Washington,' that amazing capital to the south.

I still have the picture Dad took at the Lincoln Memorial of we three brothers and, behind us, our mother — proud, hopeful, a bit worried for her sons, not knowing she had already passed on the gift."

I suspect Mom was less Republican than she was Irish. Her father, Charles Patrick Shields, was an Irish-American straight from Eugene O'Neill. Back in the 1950s, when he was working the night shift, he would head off to the plant each evening wearing his workman's cap and peacoat.

Grandpop's pride was his role as the Democratic committeeman for his neighborhood of North Philadelphia rowhouses. Long after the area began its rapid shift from Irish-American to African American, he would continue to brag about "bringing in the best division in the city."

He was, as I said, a true classic. At night after supper he would take his grandkids on long walks through the streets of North Philadelphia, through neighborhoods terribly run down and crime-ridden today. He would light up his Phillies cigar and lead us for miles. When we pleaded exhaustion, he would calmly send us back home and continue on his own. My fondest memories are of Grandpop back at his home on Fifteenth Street after our walk. He'd sit in his chair beneath the mantelpiece to read the bulldog edition of the next morning's *Inquirer*. Then, having finished the paper, he would fold it and, with a sly but approving smile, he'd look at me and announce in tones of sheer delight, "Christopher John!"

Though she might never have admitted it, Mom inherited the heart of Grandpop's Irishness. I remember coming home in the fall of 1954 and seeing the TV on. Since Mom never watched television in the daytime, it was odd to catch her following some "hearings" in Washington. Years later I would realize that what she was watching so religiously were the Army-McCarthy hearings. Joe McCarthy's Senate enemies were going after him for his intervention on behalf of a young draftee.

While these were the hearings that would bring the Wisconsin senator down, I have no doubt whom the former Mary Teresa Shields was rooting for — and, it wasn't the army. Her loyalties, as I said, were less partisan than tribal. In the case of Joe McCarthy, her conversion to Dad's Republicanism neatly coincided with her being 100 percent Irish.

Dad and Mom gave to us in ways that didn't involve money. For one thing, they paid an enormous amount of attention to what we said. Ours was a family where you were forced, on a daily basis, to explain yourself. "What's this?" my father would ask if some unfamiliar TV program was on. We knew to be ready to tell him exactly why we were watching it. "Where did you learn that?" was one of my father's favorites. "Who told you that?" was another. Whatever was said had to be defended and then annotated.

I remember hearing TV host Dick Cavett

ask John Huston what he looked for in life. The great film director, then dying of lung disease, came back with a single word: "Interest."

Politics, which has become essential to my daily life, is not an interest I was born with. Yes, I wanted to save the world at the age of five and rooted precociously for Eisenhower at six, but I was hardly what you'd call a boy political junkie. I remember one long ago Monday night in the early fifties when CBS bumped the country's highest-rated show, *I Love Lucy*, for an address by President Eisenhower. My brothers and I spent the half-hour mocking Ike's bald pate. "Old Coonskin," we kept calling him.

What recruited me, body and soul, to the political life was the 1960 race between John F. Kennedy and Richard Nixon. I have never again gotten so emotional about a political campaign.

I don't want to rehash the whole race now. I wrote a book about Jack Kennedy's and Dick Nixon's rivalry that detailed the entire saga from their strange early friendship through the feud's final showdown, when Ted Kennedy played his backroom role triggering the Watergate probe. What I didn't write in that book and what I will tell you now is whose side I ended up on.

Everyone forgets that JFK appeared on the political horizon as a shooting star. I remember the first time I heard the name "Kennedy." We were coming up the driveway to our house on Southampton Road, listening on the radio of our '54 Chevrolet Impala to what would be the last ever floor fight at a national political convention. Nominated a second time for president, former Illinois governor Adlai Stevenson had thrown the choice of his running mate open to the delegates. As we listened to the roll call, the battle for the coveted slot had narrowed to Estes Kefauver, the senator from Tennessee, who had made his name probing organized crime, and the newcomer from Massachusetts, Kennedy. Not knowing the other guy, I rooted for Kefauver, aware that I'd be cheering on Ike in the fall. I even crafted a pun for the occasion: "Keef-all-for Eisenhower."

But I soon discovered that Kennedy was a Catholic like us. Like Dad, he was a member of the Knights of Columbus, and a war hero besides. It was soon made clear that he was the best hope to nullify the country's rejection of New York governor Al Smith, the 1928 Democratic presidential nominee. His coreligionists held as a matter of faith that Smith's Roman Catholicism had been the chief reason for his defeat.

The 1960 election threatened our family with a terrible conflict between party and religion. When I asked Dad how he intended to vote, he said somewhat firmly that he was "a Republican." When I pushed the issue with Mom I could tell she was torn. As for me, I dreaded the prospect of having to go with Nixon over Kennedy. I had a large newspaper route at the time and remember my branch manager, an adult, asking me who I was for. "Kennedy in the primaries," I said tactfully. I was being Clintonesque. The whole truth was that I knew I would have to be for Nixon in November.

At fourteen, I was about to take the plunge. I was about to care about an election more than I have ever cared again. I began that summer rooting for Nixon. But when I watched every hour of the dramatic Democratic convention in Los Angeles, my loyalties shifted. I watched Eleanor Roosevelt with her high-pitched voice try to save it for her hero, Adlai, "Let it go to a second," she said from the podium. "I beseech you, let it go to a second ballot." Caught up in the glamour of the Los Angeles convention I experienced the opposite impulse. I swooned at the whole notion of a Kennedy dynasty. How great it would be, I calculated, to have Jack reign for eight years, Lyndon Johnson eight, then Bobby and Teddy for eight more each.

Ten days later I watched Nixon and Henry Cabot Lodge accept the GOP nomination in Chicago. My infatuation with the Kennedys fizzled. I became convinced that Nixon was a far more serious candidate than Kennedy, far stronger in confronting the Communists. It was not a popular position at La Salle College High School. When a teacher got the idea to poll our homeroom, the vote was twenty-four for JFK, nine for Nixon. I was surprised to learn there were even that many bucking the Catholic Kennedy tide.

My ultimate loyalty to Nixon was based on a trio of factors: We were Republicans, and Nixon looked like the stronger candidate on foreign policy. Most important, he struck me as the underdog, the plain-looking guy with no money up against the rich and handsome Jack.

The foreign policy factor was deadly serious back then. As I said in the last chapter, the late 1950s were not a good time for our side in the Cold War. The Russians were ahead in space, and, with a firm grip on Eastern Europe, they were extending their

81

reach all the way to Cuba. The big question, Nixon kept insisting, was whether the United States and the other democracies would make the same mistake they did in the late 1930s: appeasement. Kennedy always struck me as a tad vague on that point, especially when he refused during the TV debates to say whether he would send troops to repel a Red Chinese attack on the offshore islands of Quemoy and Matsu.

Exalted over this small evidence of appeasement, Nixon let him have it:

> The problem is not these two little pieces of real estate — they are unimportant. It isn't the few people who live on them — they are not too important. It's the principle involved. These two islands are in the area of freedom. I think it is shocking for a candidate for the presidency of the United States to say that he is willing to hand over a part of the Free World to the Communist world. Let me say this: If you elect me president, I assure you that I will not hand over one square foot of the Free World to the Communists.

His opponent's assault on Kennedy carried the full sound and fury of the Cold War. The contest with the Communists had taken on the rules of a board game. Every pawn they grabbed was one fewer pawn left to the Free World defenders. Every "square foot" of real estate the other side won brought them a foot closer to grabbing the ultimate prize: *us.* This is the precise thinking and rhetoric that would lead America, no matter which man won in 1960, into the morass of Vietnam. Not knowing what lay ahead, however, I saw Nixon's position as tougher and therefore smarter.

Also affecting me was the class issue. As columnist Tom Wicker would write years later, Nixon was "one of us." Like tens of millions of other Americans, the Matthewses were cloth-coat Republican. We were the people in the middle, equally remote from welfare and tax breaks. I remember a scene late in the campaign when a raincoated Nixon, his five o'clock shadow in full bloom, said witheringly, "You know it's not *Jack*'s money they're going to be spending."

For the Nixon crowd, election night proved to be a catastrophe, made all the crueler by the early projections that showed Nixon the winner. By 7:30 it was all over. Kennedy was headed for an electoral land-slide. It was the first — and last — time I have cried over an election result.

HERE'S WHAT I REALLY THINK: I think my politics are a result of where I came from. A product of the middle class, my gut impulse is to root for them politically. I care about the man or woman who gets up with the alarm clock to catch the early bus. I care about the family sweating to get the kids through college. I care about the guy who does his own taxes and does them honestly. I'm with them. I want them to know their Social Security and Medicare will be there for them when they retire. I want them to get help with college expenses. And I believe that everyone who puts in a good day's work deserves a living income, which for me includes health care. In this country, those who work should be accorded the dignity of workers.

I think Americans hate handouts. They can't stand people who condescend to them. The moment this country sees an issue in terms of the elite versus the middle class, bet on the middle class. The Equal Rights Amendment would have been ratified easily had those in the "movement" had the good sense and humility to grasp this. The Vietnam War protests might have been far more effective had they not been populated by privileged college kids bent on demonstrating their cultural and moral superiority over the "hardhats."

The Clintons — and I think Hillary, especially — never *got* it. She could have won the argument over health care if she'd made it a workplace issue rather than a welfare issue. Franklin Roosevelt knew better. He insisted that Social Security never be financed out of general revenues but out of a special "payroll tax" paid by workers and their employers. He didn't want anyone to get the idea that it was a welfare program. He wanted it to be a system that insured the retiree's dignity as well as his livelihood. He wanted Americans to know that everyone who participated in Social Security was carrying his own load.

Most people looked at Hillary's scheme as a way to skim benefits and options from the middle class and award them, free of charge, to the poor. They worried she was grabbing for their wallets.

Surrounded by a squadron of propeller-headed social theorists, people who love power without the inconvenience of an election, Hillary wanted the country to know that any benefits flowing from her health care project should be credited to one person: her. No wonder most Americans saw her scheme as a turnoff. One Evita was enough.

At the onset of the twenty-first century, this country's greatest need was to strengthen existing programs like Social Security for the long haul, basing any new commitments on the same self-help principle on which FDR relied. The great failure of the Clinton years was the failure to do just that. When we bought that "bridge to the twenty-first century" from Clinton we might as well have been buying the Brooklyn Bridge.

Hillary Clinton is a special problem. She and her crowd see themselves as a guardian class. They see their mission as molding American life according to some grand design. Down here on planet earth we get to join Hillary's health "cooperatives." She expects us to cheer her as she gets to choreograph things from above.

There's an arrogance there. It's one people can smell, and they don't like it.

JOHN F. KENNEDY

"I don't think you've ever gotten over it," Senator Daniel Patrick Moynihan said to me not long ago. And he was right. The death of John F. Kennedy had told a heretofore blessed country that it could not have the leader it had chosen.

On Nov. 22, 1963, I was a freshman at Holy Cross. It was just after lunch on Friday and I was in the basement of Kimball Hall checking my mail when a classmate burst in with the stunning and horrid news.

I headed over to my world history class, which was taught by Jim Powers. When I walked in the door, the first thing that Powers said to the class was that those who wanted to be excused could leave without being recorded with a "cut." I went immediately to the basement of Carlin Hall and turned on the TV set. Walter Cronkite was on the air, saying that Kennedy was dead. I remember how Cronkite just a few moments later took off his glasses, and I realized he was crying.

I stayed at that TV set for the longest

time. It's a truism that all of us can name where we were when we heard the news and what channel we watched. Most of us watched Cronkite's program. The astounding drama continued through the whole weekend. Holy Cross finally canceled all classes and everyone went home.

I remember that, on my way to Philadelphia, a woman on an escalator in New York asked me where I went to school. When I told her up in Massachusetts at Holy Cross, she said to me, "Well, they must be very sad up there." Of course it hadn't yet sunk in the way everyone thought it would. It could be that's the way some people deal with loss. But, in the strange ways of survivor's guilt, Kennedy's death may have been a stronger blow to those who opposed him than it was for some of his more casual supporters.

The horror in Dallas certainly took the light out of politics. What came next was a grim period in American political life. Something profound was missing. Even as I became a Goldwater enthusiast, the leader I had most wanted to spend just a few minutes with was Jack Kennedy.

There are some things I find hard to explain about myself. One is that I have never been as emotional about politics as I was the night Dick Nixon lost. And another is that I don't think I've ever felt so deadened as by the assassination of Jack Kennedy.

HERE'S WHAT I REALLY THINK: I believe that era we call "the sixties" was sparked by the grief engendered by our loss of JFK. Before, it was all dark suits, short hair, and thin ties. After, it was long hair, hard rock, and dope.

But, once the sadness began to fade, there was a stirring of new excitement in the country. By late 1967 the whole world, from Berkeley to Paris to Prague, was basking in an idealistic springtime of freedom that would be marred only by more tragedy in Memphis and Los Angeles.

CHAPTER FIVE

FREEDOM IS CONTAGIOUS

WHEN AN AMERICAN SAYS THAT HE LOVES
HIS COUNTRY, HE MEANS THAT HE LOVES AN
INNER AIR, AN INNER LIGHT IN WHICH
FREEDOM LIVES AND IN WHICH A MAN CAN
DRAW THE BREATH OF SELF-RESPECT.

ADLAI STEVENSON

If I can't insist you agree with everything — or anything — I say, I ask only that you believe my words and emotions are my own. The Chris Matthews you see and hear is the only one there is. Fred O'Regan, my friend since we served together in the Peace Corps, lifts my spirits whenever he says I haven't changed in the thirty years since we've been back from Swaziland.

Freedom is where my politics begin and end. To me it's not just some word engraved in marble, but that "inner light" Stevenson so eloquently invoked.

On my way home from Africa thirty years ago, I had a revealing glimpse into how the Third World really views the United States. With little money in my pocket, I needed to live frugally. Because of how I traveled and where I stayed, I could meet ordinary folks and listen to them. I could ask them questions and answer theirs. It was quite a lesson.

On Zanzibar, I met a young Indian in his late teens who grabbed at the chance to tell a young American what life was like for him on this exotic but appalling island. Regimentation was absolute, whether it applied to hair length or courtship. Even holding hands in public was forbidden. Being an Indian, this young man could not engage in business. Nor could he leave the island.

The only refuge for this lonely victim of repression was his small apartment, which he had transformed into a shrine to anything American. The walls were covered with posters and album covers of Jimi Hendrix and the Rolling Stones. It was his own little island to which he had transported the culture and freedom of a far-off land. He could not wait to get me into his tiny temple of rebellion.

I'd experienced this before, this devotion to America from afar. Before the fall of

1968, when our Peace Corps group arrived there, Swaziland had been the last British colony in Africa. I worked with many expatriates who had spent careers in the colonial service and then had stayed on to work for the newly independent government. They were devoted to such icons of Hollywood as Fred Astaire and Ginger Rogers and retained their regard for the "Yanks," their World War II allies. It was fascinating to me to see this wonder they felt toward a country that spoke the same language but who enjoyed freedoms much more *real* than the class-ridden variety they had left behind.

And I had seen the love that desperate black South Africans, struggling under the historic weight of apartheid, felt for anything American, particularly jazz, that freest of all musical forms. For these men, aspiration and freedom were synonymous with that Promised Land across the Atlantic.

What we often can't see from the vantage point of home is that our country's greatest influence in the world is exerted not by diplomats in pinstriped suits but by freedom-loving Americans in blue jeans. What people find irresistible about us is not liberty in the abstract but what comes of it: the music, the clothes, the attitude. This is also, we've learned to our horror, what others find dangerous.

There is a wonderful bit of dialogue in Paul Mazursky's movie *Moscow on the Hudson.* It comes when a couple of CIA bureacrats are grilling the young Soviet musician played by Robin Williams on his reasons for seeking asylum:

"Why are you defecting?" an agent demands.

"Freedom."

"Artistic freedom or political freedom."

"Freedom."

Like the Eskimo who has thirteen different words for snow, we Americans make an art of subtle distinctions. Those who see the wonder of snow for the first time just want to go sledding.

In 1989 I had the privilege of snagging a ringside seat at the greatest explosion of freedom in my lifetime — the fall of the Iron Curtain. My personal brush with this extraordinary epoch began with an April visit to Hungary. This, remember, was the courageous country we had watched stand alone against Warsaw Pact tanks with nothing but the cobblestones from the streets and the occasional Molotov cocktail. Now, years later, I had read reports of a "reform movement" and jumped at the chance to learn about it firsthand.

Upon my arrival in Budapest I quickly was able to see that here was a country straining from its East European imprisonment to join the West. The elevator at the Intercontinental Hotel rose and fell to the Beach Boys. The sidewalk caricaturists favored Woody Allen, Humphrey Bogart, and Marilyn Monroe.

The pull of political freedom was equally manifest. On the wall of the government public information agency was tacked a wire-service photo showing Erich Honecker, the East German dictator, standing directly in front of some deer antlers. It was no accident that this image — the Communist boss looked as if he had horns — was the slyly chosen pinup.

Before leaving Washington I had gotten the name of an economics professor, Geza Jeszenszky, who was a leader in Democratic Forum, the rump faction working to overthrow the creaky Communist regime. He lived in an old, high-ceilinged apartment building reminiscent of *The Third Man.* While his wife, also a professor, treated my six-year-old son, Michael, to crayons and paper in the next room, the soft-spoken Jeszenszky hosted a pipe-smoking British journalist and me to tea, biscuits, and a briefing on the incredible work in which he and his allies were engaged.

Calmly and confidently, he described the meetings the forum was holding "in the countryside." We learned about the "writers and intellectuals" attending these meetings. Our host insisted that after all the years of Communist repression and all the failed attempts to change things, this time was different. He spoke of the morale boost he and his fellow activists got from watching Russian Boris Yeltsin stand up to the Kremlin bosses on TV. "Freedom is contagious," he said.

Yes, it is. That September a new Hungarian government ripped down the barbed wire on its western frontier, allowing twelve thousand East Germans to flee its borders. With that miraculous act of political courage, the Iron Curtain was relegated to history's dustbin. Within the year, the country had adopted a new constitution and held free elections: Hungary was now a democratic republic and that hopeful professor with whom I had shared tea and sympathy was its foreign minister.

In November I stood in a cold drizzle on the East Berlin side of the Brandenburg Gate. The previous Saturday the faltering Communist government had allowed its people to pass through the Wall for the first time since its crude construction in 1961. A rumor was spreading that the gate itself, so long a symbol of the city's tragic bifurcation, was about to open.

Moving through the throngs of excited East Berliners, I began asking everyone with whom I could make eye contact what that word, "freedom," meant to them. *"Was ist freiheit?"* I asked in my extremely limited German. *What is freedom?* Slowly a crowd began to gather around me. In the rain and gloom of a November night, I suddenly had stirred the kind of exuberant give-and-take you now see regularly on *Hardball.*

"We really do believe in democracy," a woman pleaded, as if she were speaking through me to the entire Free World. "Let us have a chance!"

Next I asked a young man what kind of system did he want, capitalist or socialist? "We want a united Germany where the people can make the choice," he answered. "We want a socialist country," insisted another.

Then a young woman suggested a mix: Western-style economic freedoms combined with "the caring for the people" of socialist countries. "I want the freedom to earn what I have worked for and not be forced to do something because I am told to," another man said, as I continued scribbling in my notebook.

Finally, I heard the defining statement journalists wait a lifetime to record. *This* is *freiheit!*" said a serious young man in an army surplus jacket. "This standing in a public place arguing openly about such things as democracy, capitalism, and socialism."

"Four weeks ago, we couldn't have done this!" a woman chimed in.

"It is fun being in the same decade with you," President Roosevelt cabled his World War II ally Winston Churchill in 1942. While television talk show hosts operate on a somewhat less majestic plane of history, those are my exact sentiments toward John McLaughlin. Early in 1988 he began inviting me on his wildly popular *The McLaughlin Group.* By then, everyone I knew in Washington was watching this lively look at the country's politics.

John runs the *Group* with the same tyrannical ego that a pre–Vatican II New England Jesuit — which he once was — rules over a classroom. What makes it fun is the self-satire, which I've never been sure John intends. Pretending to *La Bohème,* the show often ends up the practiced equivalent of the Marx Brothers in *Night at the Opera.* What makes it a great mix of scuttlebutt and entertainment is its zany ground speed. Of all John's familiar lines, none is more exhilarating than, "Okay, let's get out of it." By keeping the show moving, John manages to offer a weekly syllabus on the national political buzz without wasting anyone's time.

Rivaling P. T. Barnum in showmanship, John is also a fabulous traveling partner. He was my companion in those historic days when the Berlin Wall opened and the Iron Curtain was in the process of crashing down.

We began our excursion into history on a promontory above the Potsdamerplatz, the checkpoint the Berlin authorities had decided to open for the day. Through the wall poured a long, grim line of East Berliners looking every bit like people from a black-and-white movie marching onto a Technicolor movie screen. Awaiting the one-day visitors from the East were a number of West German commercial trucks, each dispensing free samples. The one closest to the wall was marked "Bahlsen Biscuits." From its open back some guy was handing small packages to the trudging line of East Berliners.

"This is where forty years of Stalinism has gotten them," said our disgusted West German driver, "standing in line for biscuits."

This being the British occupation sector, fatigue-wearing soldiers from the UK were ladling out coffee from army-green jeep cans. "Poor *devils*," John whispered, in his best imitation of a stiff-upper-lip British accent.

The next day we took a wild excursion into Communist East Germany. Our first stop that Sunday morning was Potsdam, scene of the Big Three summit in June 1945. It was here that Roosevelt had gained Stalin's backing for the final move against Japan. A souvenir pamphlet described how the United States had dropped the atom bombs on Hiroshima and Nagasaki in order to "rule the world." I noticed that the propaganda marked the beginning of the "anti-Hitler coalition" at 1941, the year Hitler attacked the Soviet Union. It recounted the Nazi capitulation to a Red Army field marshal in 1945. It made no reference to the western front of the war or to any general named Eisenhower.

John and I went on to Wittenberg, the cathedral where Martin Luther had tacked the ninety-five theses on the door in 1517. The only sign that this is a major landmark of western civilization were the words *"Ein Vester Borg ist unser Gott"* on a banner wrapped around the spire. Later I found John in the dim sanctuary standing on the tomb of Luther, the man who had stood against the power of the papacy, indeed, against the entire European order of his time. "How did he know?" he asked me gravely.

That evening we drove through Weimar, home to the country's brief post–World War I effort at democracy. The pollution from the lignite stoves was so dense that we needed to close the windows of our car and turn on the air-conditioning full blast.

Then, on to Buchenwald. We arrived at the death camp a half-hour after sunset. Searching among the shadowy buildings, we came across an elderly custodian. With the help of my press credentials we got him to open up some of the buildings.

The entire compound was a monument to Communism. Every cell displayed a fresh wreath sent from the various Communist parties of Europe: Belgian, Dutch, etc. The weary, plump little man unlocked the door to one ramshackle shed and showed us the room where six thousand Soviet soldiers had been killed. He explained to us in ghastly detail how the Nazis had gotten the young Soviet soldiers to take seats, ostensibly in preparation for medical exams, and then had fired through a narrow slit in the wall and blown out their brains.

"Were any *Jews* killed here?" John inquired, cutting through the government-issued talking points. I could not decipher the old man's mumbled response.

In Leipzig we stopped at St. Nicholas Church, on whose organ Johann Sebastian Bach had first played many of his chorales. It was now home to the "peace vigils" that lent a powerful moral glow to the burgeoning reform movement. We had supper in the Auerbacher Keller where Goethe had eaten and set a scene in *Faust*. The Germany of a great cultural tradition was about to be liberated from sixty years of Nazi and Communist repression.

I need to give credit to the two people who most shaped my heartfelt opinions on freedom. The first is a political figure from whom, ironically, Hillary Clinton and I both got our first *philosophical* interest in politics: the father of the modern conservative movement, Arizona senator Barry Goldwater. I listened to his speech at the 1960 Republican Convention on the radio at my grandmother's house. Before that election I had never heard of the "conservative" philosophy he preached, but it would soon become a big part of my life. With the 1960 election lost and JFK in the White House, I emerged as a Goldwaterite all the way. It was his philosophy of individual freedom and his opposition to any government measure that restricted such freedom that appealed to me.

During the next few years, I would not only understand what these "conservatives" were all about, I would become one. Soon I was a regular reader of William F. Buckley, Jr.'s *National Review*. My friend Tim Urbanski and I knew the suburban Philadelphia drugstores where it would arrive first each month.

What we adherents liked about Goldwater conservatism was quite clear. The senator from Arizona advocated a maximum degree of personal freedom. That meant minimum government: Protect the country, deliver the mail, and follow the Constitution, then get out of our lives. Forget "me-too Republicanism." Nixon had tried that, and it had failed.

The other influence on me back then was closer to home. He was my high-school teacher, Gerald Tremblay.

The adventures I detail in this book might not have occurred were it not for Tremblay, who taught English at La Salle College High School, in Philadelphia. It's because of him that I began writing regularly, discovered the allure of New York and the wide door it opens to American culture, and most important, gained confidence in myself.

"Tremblay." That's what we called him when he was not around. He was the first person I knew who had a foreign car, driving a VW bug in an era of station wagons. He was into Broadway, into Shakespeare, into all the American novelists he thought were any good.

It was the fall of 1962, my senior year of high school, and I had begun contributing articles to the school newspaper, *The Wisterian*. Perhaps more important, I also had begun to hang around the paper's office after school. It was a bastion of creative youth, decorated by a small phonograph with a single 45-rpm record, "Silver Dagger" by a new folk singer named Joan Baez, which we played over and over.

"If you're going to hang around every day," Tremblay said to me one memorable afternoon, "you might as well be an editor!" I thereby became one of the newspaper's two assistant editors. Not only was it a real status boost over playing in the school band, I began to realize a passion that I still practice: writing. I remember one time in the newsroom I announced, "I do all the grassroots writing around here." Tremblay immediately replied, "Yeah, you know what's in the grassroots . . . bullshit."

Even more valuable than the status was the opportunity my new position gave me to spend time with Tremblay. I had never met anyone like him. In a suburban, climbing world, he didn't think money was important. His preference was for the latest author he'd discovered, the latest Broadway play he planned to see, the latest thinker whose ideas impressed him. His views on politics could be reduced to a single word: balance. When the country tilted too far right, we needed to move left. When it tilted too far to the left, he pushed in the opposite direction. The older I get, the more I buy this very American way of looking at things.

The spring of my senior year brought with it several big events in my life. The first was the trip to New York, site of the Columbia University convention, for high-school newspaper editors. In a single weekend we took the Staten Island Ferry for five cents, visited the Empire State Building, ate at Mama Leone's, wandered through the old

Barnes & Noble warehouse, and saw three Broadway plays: *A Man for All Seasons*, *Stop the World — I Want To Get Off*, and *A Thousand Clowns*. We also saw two foreign movies: *La Dolce Vita* and *Last Year at Marienbad*. One of us was even lucky enough to get propositioned by a pimp. "I got what you want: white, Spanish, or colored." I came home with a reproduction of the "Mona Lisa" and a paperback on Thomas Jefferson. What we did not do was attend a single event at the Columbia University high-school newspaper editors' convention.

Whenever people bring up the subject of inspiring teachers, I know that I had one of the best. Gerald Tremblay took a suburban kid from Philadelphia and showed him a magnificent world of culture and ideas where the scorecard didn't involve money or the size of the car you drive. Life's success, he taught me, was measured *within*.

Tremblay was responsible for another milestone during my senior year — the founding of *The Gazebo*, the new La Salle literary magazine. Even though his own preference was for balance, that didn't mean he was intolerant of his students' enthusiasms. He encouraged me to produce an essay on the foundations of conservatism.

105

With apologies to Edmund Burke, below is some evidence of my adolescent capacity for deep thought:

"The early realization of man that he was an imperfect being led him to the formation of certain principles. It was in the formation of these principles that led to the earliest foundations of conservative philosophy.

Ironically, it was the great upheavals of the late eighteenth century which gave this philosophy its fullest meaning and significance. To understand this, we must first investigate and then contrast two revolutions of the century.

Under the banner of liberty, equality, and fraternity the people of France overthrew the government in 1790, murdered the monarch and all the members of the ruling class. For these same noble goals, apparently, these free people named a man absolute dictator for life — Napoleon Bonaparte — and thus turned over all chance of the freedom of which they had spoken so highly.

During this same century, the American colonies, because of excessive taxes and a desire for independence, forcefully separated themselves from their mother country. In sharp contrast to the short-sighted, short-lived First Republic of France, the American democrats had within ten years ratified a constitution of principles which guaranteed the preservation of the freedom of the individual that it fought so hard to achieve. The results of this deed are, in essence, the triumph of conservatism. Where the emotions of the mob had failed to obtain freedom for the individual, *the goal of all government,* set principles have succeeded."

Pretty lofty notions for a fourteen-year-old.

My biggest honor that last year at La Salle came when I was invited to compete on the school's College Bowl team. That, too, contained a harbinger of things to come. Modeled after the GE-sponsored TV show, it pitted a panel of four La Salle students against four from another Christian Brothers school, West Catholic. While our rival picked its team based on grade point average, La Salle picked its panel in an open competition. Three of the selectees were brilliant, National Merit scholar types. The fourth was *me*.

I can still remember three of the toss-up questions to which I beat everyone else with the answer.

Q: Who was the Norwegian who revolutionized the drama in the late nineteenth century?

Answer: Henrik Ibsen.

Q: Who was the philosopher that combined mathematics and geometry?

A: Descartes.

Q: What year was the so-called "disputed election" and who were the presidential candidates?

A: 1876; Rutherford B. Hayes and Samuel Tilden.

This was in 1963. Thirty-seven years later I found myself making frequent references to that once singular "disputed election" when our country found itself embroiled for five weeks in another.

HERE'S WHAT I REALLY THINK: I think freedom is this country's greatest gift to the world. In the political arena, it's the ability of the American people to do what they're *not supposed to.* And as everyone can tell, I relish *my* freedom to think and speak out loud on national television five nights a week. Sometimes I relish it too much. You should know that at such moments *Hardball*'s executive producer, Phil Griffin, is shouting, "Punch!!!" in my earpiece. That's our agreed-upon cue for, "Chris, you're talking too much; please stop now!"

But as that young man in East Berlin so poignantly declared, true freedom is the guaranteed *right* to open discourse and uninhibited debate. This is what we try and do each night on *Hardball*.

WINSTON CHURCHILL

"There but for the grace of God," he said of one rival, "goes God." He called another "a modest man with much to be modest about," still another, "a sheep in sheep's clothing."

"You are my fifth favorite actor," he greeted a star of the British stage. "The first four are the *Marx Brothers!*" "If I were your wife, I'd put poison in your coffee," a tart-tongued gentlewoman scolded him. "If I were your husband," he shot back, "I'd drink it."

What guest would I most like to host on *Hardball?* My resounding answer is Sir Winston Spencer Churchill, whom I believe to be the greatest man of the twentieth century.

In fact, before the twentieth century began, he'd proven himself both as a soldier and as a war correspondent. Upon graduating from the Royal Military Academy at Sandhurst, Britain's West Point equivalent, Churchill went to India, where he saw action on the northwest frontier, an episode that later provided the background for his first book on military tactics, *The Story of the Malakand Field Force.*

He next joined General Kitchener's campaign to retake Khartoum from the Islamic zealots led by the Mahdi. This gave young Winston a chance to ride in the last cavalry charge by the British army. The book arising from this experience was *The River War,* in which this junior officer dared to criticize his superior for desecrating the Mahdi's tomb.

In 1899, Churchill ran for Parliament for the first time and lost. Undaunted, he then set off for the Boer War as a newspaper correspondent. Captured by the enemy, he managed to climb over a latrine wall, hide himself on a train, and escape over the border to Mozambique. Safely back in Cape Town, he regained his commission in the army and returned to the fighting, indeed, to the exact spot where he'd been captured.

Churchill arrived in London as a hero. This time he stood for Parliament and won. As a member of the House of Commons, he exhibited the same audacity he had in battle, the same independence he'd displayed in writing about it. In his maiden address he attacked his own party's defense budget, the same act of rebellion that had cost his father, Randolph, his career. When his own Conservative allies turned sharply protectionist, moreover, Churchill didn't hesitate to quit the party and join the free-trader Liberals.

As first lord of the admiralty in World War I, his taste for free thinking proved calamitous. In a bid to end the trench warfare in France he advocated a combined land and sea campaign through the Dardanelles. The idea was to grab Constantinople, thereby robbing Germany of its Turkish ally. But only a half-hearted version of the plan was enacted, disaster was the result, and its author took full blame. With his reputation scarred and his position as first lord lost, Churchill rejoined the army and headed for France. Having failed in his plan to end the bloody war in the trenches, he would take his place there.

The man never quit. With the popularity of socialism on the rise after the war. Churchill lost three straight elections. Rather than sink into political irrelevance with the Liberal party, now unable to compete with the new, left-leaning Labour party, he rejoined the Conservatives. It's one thing to *"rat,"* he gleefully confessed, it's another to *"rerat."*

In word as well as in deed, Churchill took charge of his own destiny. Again, he placed himself at the center of the action. "I am immersed in Winston's biography," a senior colleague said of *The World Crisis*, his first work on World War I, "disguised as a history of the universe."

Although he was wrong about many things in his long career — he was slow to accept both women's suffrage and India's independence — he would be proven right about the big ones.

A man who lost a half a dozen elections in his life, he had nothing but contempt for those who loved the word "democracy" but rejected free elections. "Democracy is not some harlot in the street to be picked up by some man with a Tommy gun," he said. "Democracy is based on reason, a sense of fair play, and freedom and a respect for other people."

Churchill probably drank too much. He most certainly lived the life of an aristocrat, never, ever, venturing into a kitchen or traveling, even to war, without a valet. But he paid for his extravagances himself, supporting his taste for luxury with his verbal eloquence. He made his living, as he put it, by his "pen" and by his "tongue." His daughter Mary recalled her family living "literally from book to book and from one article to the next."

One of my favorite images of him, drawn by his premier American biographer, William Manchester, is of Churchill climbing the stairs at midnight, after seeing his overnight guests to their rooms as he went off to dictate and edit well into the morning.

How can you not be impressed with this man? Winston Churchill would have been one of the great men of his age even if he had *not* done what he did. What he did was save the honor of the twentieth century.

Starting in 1933, the year Adolf Hitler came to power in Germany, Churchill was right about the Nazi threat when others, especially the Conservatives, were wrong. He saw Germany building both its military machine and its concentration camps. When war came, he had the credentials to face down Adolf Hitler and to say Britain would "never" surrender. Churchill's forty years as a fighter, especially those when he fought alone in the 1930s, were his job application.

In 1935, Hitler renewed military conscription in Germany and proclaimed the Luftwaffe now the match of the Royal Air Force. But when Churchill warned that the Germans were building 150 planes a month, he was accused of "scaremongering." In 1936, Hitler marched his armies into the Rhineland, an area demilitarized after World War I. Watching from London, British prime minister Stanley Baldwin told his country it had nothing to fear from Germany. Why should the British care if the Nazis grabbed a few countries on their way to fighting the Bolsheviks in Russia?

In January 1937, Britain's new prime minister, Neville Chamberlain, offered to appease Hitler by handing over a few colonies in Africa. Churchill's judgment: "This has been a good week for dictators."

He then predicted: "The day will come when at some point or another, you will have to take a stand, and I pray to God when that day comes that we may not find, through an unwise policy, that we have to make that stand alone."

A month later, Hitler marched into Austria. A year later, at Munich, the world watched as Prime Minister Chamberlain handed over much of Czechoslovakia to Hitler. At home the British people counted him a hero. Bucking public opinion, Churchill called the giveaway a "total and unmitigated defeat." He sought to relay the truth to his countrymen, not court their favor. "And do not suppose that this is the end," he warned the House of Commons. "This is only the beginning of the reckoning."

On September 1, 1939, claiming Germany had been invaded, Hitler responded by crossing the border into Poland. The Second World War had begun. Churchill, reinstated as first lord of the admiralty, broadcast to America his view of those countries that remained neutral: "Each one hopes that if he feeds the crocodile enough, the crocodile will eat him last."

In May, Churchill became Britain's prime minister, on the same day that Hitler launched his *blitz* across Europe. With Holland, Denmark, and Belgium overrun and France, England's last ally, about to sign an armistice, and with a quarter-million British troops, the country's entire army, stranded at the French port city of Dunkirk, Churchill still refused to quit.

"Of course, whatever happens in Dunkirk," he told his cabinet, "we shall fight on."

Even in England's hour of peril Churchill was brutally candid. "Even if, which I do not for a moment believe, this island, or a large part of it, were subjugated and starving," he told the British people, laying out the worst, "then our empire beyond the seas, armed and guarded by the British fleet, would carry on the struggle until, in God's good time, the New World, with all its power and might, steps forth to the rescue and liberation of the old."

No leader was ever so clear-eyed about the villains he stood against. An instinctive anti-Communist, he understood nevertheless that it was Hitler's Nazism that posed the immediate danger. "We have but one aim, and one single irrevocable purpose," he said after Hitler's invasion of Russia in 1941. "We are resolved to destroy Hitler and every vestige of the Nazi regime. From this nothing will turn us, nothing. We will never parlay, we will never negotiate with Hitler or any of his gang. Any man or state who fights against Nazidom will have our aid. Any man or state who marches with Hitler is our foe." He said the same in private. "If Hitler invaded hell," he told his private secretary, John Colville, "I would make at least a favorable reference to the Devil in the House of Commons."

Churchill was equally alert to the post–World War II threat of Communism. At Yalta in February 1945, he alone pushed for free elections in Poland. Sick, wearied by the war, and tragically unwary of the new global menace from the left, Franklin Roosevelt felt he could rely on the old charm; he could "handle" Stalin. In his view, free elections in Poland were a "distant" concern for the United States. To Churchill, the issue of free elections remained paramount. When Stalin broke his promise to hold them, Churchill saw the writing on the wall.

He would have to do so as leader of the opposition. Once again, Churchill had to suffer the cruel indignity that democracy demands of those who seek elective office. He was called home from his meeting with Stalin and Truman at Potsdam to accept his party's defeat at the polls.

Once again, Churchill made the best of it, offering a finer, more courageous vision from the opposition benches than the world was getting from those running the government. Accepting an invitation from Truman to visit his home state of Missouri, Churchill gave the speech at Westminster College that gave the "Iron Curtain" its name.

From his first electoral defeat in 1899 to his harshest defeat at the very hour of military victory in 1945, he lived out that defining fact of democracy: *You win some; you lose some.* The politician who sticks to his principles will know both. "Courage for some sudden act, maybe in the heat of battle, we all respect," his young ally Anthony Eden observed, "but there is that still rarer courage which can sustain repeated disappointment, unexpected failure, and shattering defeat. Churchill had that too, and had need of it, not for a day, but for weeks and months and years."

That's what made this man, whom the British people returned to the premiership in 1951.

A Canadian pollster, Allen Gregg, once told me that there are three elements to political success in any country: motive, passion, and spontaneity. To lead you must know where you're leading. If a politician cannot tell you on the spot why he or she is there, they shouldn't be there.

And if a politician lacks true feeling about his country and his cause, we must wonder why he or she seeks office in the first place. As for the spontaneity factor, let's just say that Winston Churchill would not be at home among today's politicians. He would have kept his cigar lit in the White House, whatever the prevailing sanctions. He would have loathed the company of politicians with every position pretested and prescripted.

When other politicians would cling to office, he was never afraid to fling it away, to risk popular rejection — which came to him on so many cruel occasions — or to start all over again. He didn't worry what his critics thought, didn't ask what someone else's definition of "is" was. He wrote his own speeches because no one else but him had the sentiment, the knowledge, the passion, or the wit to write for Winston Churchill.

The goal of World War II, this great man said, was "to revive the status of man." He wanted to raise up the individual beyond the reach of the Hitlers and Stalins of this world. His life stands as an example of what a free man can be.

CHAPTER SIX

COMMON GROUND

WE DO NOT DO WHAT WE WANT AND YET
WE ARE RESPONSIBLE FOR WHAT WE ARE.
THAT IS THE FACT.

JEAN-PAUL SARTRE

I will now tell you when and why I became a Democrat.

My two teenaged sons are fascinated with the sixties. Maybe it's that their own time is too caught up in being politically correct. They have to look to my era for charismatic outlaws such as Dennis Hopper and Keith Richards. Or maybe it's simply because they respond to the delight in my eyes, the giggle in my voice every time I reach back to those wild, intoxicating days.

How can we treasure memories from that decade of drugs and demonstrations and assassinations? The truth is, just like everyone else of my generation, I do. There was a bite in the air back then, a sweetness and a craziness. I was at the University of North Carolina, a grad student in economics, in the fall of 1967. Economics was the most practical major I could justify given the times. Everyone cool was taking philosophy or going to Yale for theology. We dismissed law school, and business school even more, as "shop," hopelessly bourgeois. What ideas, what concepts did you deal with in those little career-builders?

It was at Chapel Hill that I heard a fellow grad student, well-groomed in a blue denim work shirt and shined combat boots, refer to "the fascists" backing the Vietnam War effort. It was the first time I ever heard anyone employ this alien-sounding word in casual conversation. He was hardly alone in such ideological self-importance, "fascists." I remember some guy shouting, "No pictures" at an antiwar meeting, as if J. Edgar Hoover himself, given the necessary evidence, was poised to swoop in the door and arrest this dangerous cell of grad school types and assistant professors of psychology.

In October I made my way to the March on the Pentagon, that first big antiwar demonstration. The mall was a sea of protesters. Socialists and worse were handing out their tired appeals, screeds made suddenly more sprightly by "the movement." This was the giant pink umbrella of which they dreamed. And everywhere there were wholesome marchers: nuns, mothers with baby carriages. Accompanying it all was this joyous sense of festivity. It was an Indian summer day with the smell of trampled grass filling the air, and what was happening was a real jamboree of popular indignation.

I was not so much a demonstrator myself as an attendee. I have a clear recollection of strolling across Memorial Bridge on the other sidewalk from the marchers. I was there to see, not to do, and I preferred to keep a useful distance. Yet, despite my studied nonalignment, I could not help meeting up with the ugly side of such a demonstration.

As the crowd reached the Pentagon lawn, regiments of National Guardsmen moved forward to meet us. In a sequence of impressive, awful maneuvers, the military force took up positions along a perimeter that put them face-to-face with the arriving throng of protesters. For the first time in my life I knew the sense of being in a mob as I found myself urging the crowd to charge. The sight of all that force amassed against us — Lyndon Johnson's answer to the country's unrest radicalized me, if only temporarily.

The great news was that while we were marching, Eugene McCarthy was preparing to run against Johnson for the nomination. He was soon to become a household name. Every night I would troop over to the student affairs building to watch Walter Cronkite and Eric Sevareid narrate the ongoing saga of Clean Gene's uphill challenge to a sitting president. When he won 42 percent compared to the 49 percent Johnson won entirely on write-ins, the press declared him the victor.

Then, Robert Kennedy joined the race, which really heated things up. You were either a "McCarthy" person or a "Bobby" person. It became an enduring intramural struggle. To this day I'm curious to know which side a person was on.

I will always be grateful to Eugene McCarthy. He was an Irish-Catholic, a politician, an intellectual, and a wit. No matter that he was incapable of leading his "children's crusade" to victory in '68, he deserves historic credit for having shown young people like me that someone in power cared about the consequences of that horrible war. But I also owe him something more personal. I think it must have been he who reawoke my delight in politics that had died in Dallas. He was a man of reason, of deliberation, and of maddeningly good humor. He was the kind of Democrat I could see myself becoming.

I was deep in the stacks of the UNC library in April of '68 when a friend walked up to me to tell me that Martin Luther King had been murdered. I was visiting Montreal the night of the California primary. By then I was rooting for Bobby. I had realized Mc-Carthy was not going to beat the prowar Hubert Humphrey. But Kennedy at least had a chance. I remember waking up at about 1:30 that morning and turning on the radio to learn that Bobby had won. But then, for some reason, the networks seemed to be replaying the horror of Dallas five years earlier. Then it hit me: This was in *real* time. Robert Kennedy had been shot and was in critical condition.

On the way to the airport the next morning, the Canadian cab driver kept repeating, "The giant has stubbed his toe." The horrid act of a Palestinian nationalist had unleashed this man's own repressed nationalism.

Back at my apartment in Chapel Hill, I was glued to the television, watching the postmortems and funeral. I can't recall a day so grim as when that train carrying

Bobby and his family rolled mournfully from New York to Washington. Jack's death had held a certain terrible beauty, but Bobby's was a tragedy without grace.

In August the Democratic convention in Chicago proved to be one of the great broadcast events of all time. My roommates and I watched it gavel-to-gavel. I remember Cronkite signing off one night, telling us all to get some sleep, promising he'd be back again with continuing coverage at 10:30 the next morning. It was as if Uncle Walter was tucking us all in for the night.

I had a personal interest in that convention. The Tet offensive had displayed the enemy's unrelenting strength. In response, General William Westmoreland had asked for yet another two hundred fifty thousand troops. Since we were unable to win the war, we were going to have to sacrifice more lives just to keep from losing it.

By now my student deferment had elapsed. Johnson's "moratorium" had given us just one year of grad school. I knew I was now 1-A, directly on the firing line.

I'd made a list of possible options inside and outside the military. The only one I liked said "Peace Corps."

When I finished my two months of training near Baton Rouge, Louisiana, I headed for my assignment in Swaziland, a newly independent kingdom in southern Africa, where I was to run a small-business development program. As I was preparing to depart for training, I went out to catch all the new movies, especially *The Graduate*. Remember when the family friend counsels Dustin Hoffman to think "plastics"? Laughing at that kind of crass mentality was what the sixties were all about. Ideas — and ideals — were what was important.

Of course, as I was poised to leave the country, I also needed to check my own values. Was I going to Africa because I wanted to help Africans? Or just to beat the draft? As pathetic as it may seem today, my symbolic answer was to respond to a call for a blood donation for a young African-American hemophiliac. It may not seem like a big deal, but then again, I am the kind of person who almost faints at the sight of any blood.

I was leaving the country at a moment when people my age felt that they could make a difference. The civil rights bill had just been passed. The antiwar movement was still optimistic, its demonstrators against our entanglement in Vietnam, not against America itself.

I myself was headed for the adventure of a

lifetime. Remember what Ernest Hemingway wrote about spending his twenties in Paris? For the Peace Corps volunteers who served with me, Swaziland has been our "moveable feast." I savor the memories. Before I left I voted in my first presidential election. I would never face a tougher choice. While I thought Nixon would be more effective in extricating us from the war, I also felt Humphrey deserved credit for his early commitment to civil rights. And I liked his vice-presidential running mate, the cerebral Edmund Muskie of Maine. He reminded me of McCarthy. I voted for Humphrey.

On my last day in New York, my new Peace Corps comrade, John Catanese, and I went to see *Hair*. It was a hot ticket, and we were lucky to find seats for the Wednesday matinee. Though they were far back in the balcony, I remember seeing well enough to fall big for this seductive actress who played Sheila. Someone later pointed out that she was the only girl who didn't take off her clothes. It was Diane Keaton. It was a nice way to leave America.

Whenever people ask me about Africa, I always start with the story of the black mamba. I had heard tales of how this incredible snake could move at thirty miles an hour, how it could catch a horse on the run. I knew that its venom attacked the nervous system, that you had about fifteen minutes once it got you. I knew that, unlike other snakes, it didn't spiral horizontally but rather vertically. I had heard stories about the mamba jumping into the back of moving station wagons. I had heard the Swazis warn us not to let it get ahead of us in the veld because it strikes backward.

All this prepared me for that moment one hot afternoon, riding through the Grand Valley, a place that Catanese, who was stationed there as a rural development adviser, called "the Valley of the Doomed." I was driving a British-made Ford Escort. That meant that I was sitting on the right side. Rhodes Nhumalo, head of the Swazi Chamber of Commerce, was in the passenger's seat to my left. Gary Rowse, another volunteer, was in the backseat directly behind me.

Did I mention it was hot? Let's just say it was the first time I ever saw heat waves rising up from a *dirt* highway. We were driving along when I suddenly spotted a dark line up ahead. It was about six feet long. It seemed to stretch halfway across the road. Its head was positioned right at the exact spot I was careening toward at fifty miles an hour. Suddenly, as I was about to pass it, the snake rose on its tail, reaching right to my open window. Flinching, I veered the car over to the left. All I could think was that the serpent was in the backseat.

Gary, a good friend for thirty years who died last year, had the more dramatic view. When I'd started breathing again, he told me that the force of the car whizzing past had flipped the snake backward. I never again doubted a mamba story. That thing could *move!*

Swaziland is a little country squeezed between South Africa and Mozambique. It's divided into three elevations: high-veld, which is mountainous: low-veld, which is desert and looks like the Africa of Tarzan movies; and middle-veld, which is somewhere in between. Spend any time in Africa and you learn that it's the altitude that decides the temperature. You want to be as high as possible.

Nhlangano, the old Afrikaner village where I was posted, was middle-veld. It looked like the town in a Western. Five or six buildings lined each side of the street: a post office, a Barclay's Bank, a butcher shop, a general store, a police station.

I was escorted to Nhlangano by Simon Xhumalo, minister of commerce, industry, and mines. He gave me two explicit instructions. The first was to "develop the province." His second was, "You are not to eat at the hotel. You are to make your own meals." To Simon Xhumalo, that little hotel held bad memories of colonialism — though not bad enough to keep *him* from having lunch there that day.

That night, my first in Africa alone, I stayed in my temporary housing, the assistant district commissioner's house. It was very nice, having been built for young servants of the British Empire out on their first colonial posting. Though there was no electric power in Nhlangano, the house had a wood furnace, which I used to heat up a bath. As I was chopping the wood, a couple of Swazi kids came up to me and asked for a job. I think it was at about that time, grasping the remoteness of the spot, that I came to grips with how completely alone I truly was. All of a sudden I was in Africa, in the middle of nowhere, with no other Americans anywhere around.

Walking down the street later that afternoon, I came upon an older white man, Mr. Dye, who told me that he ran the hotel, the Robin Inn. He said that if I ever got lonely just to come by and say hello. But for the next several days I mainly kept to myself, listening to my shortwave radio as the sun went down, savoring broadcasts from the Voice of America and the BBC. Then, like a deus ex machina, company arrived. Cliff Sears, an architect from Chicago, had been assigned to design a community center nearby. The first thing he said was, "We are eating at the hotel tonight." Thank God he had had none of my Catholic school squeamishness.

My attitude toward the commerce minister's first decree was more respectful. My interpretation of his instruction that I "develop" a fourth of his country was to do what I'd been sent to do: Visit the two hundred or so small traders in the province and help them improve their businesses. But as was common with many Peace Corps programs, the host government had bit off more than it could chew. The deal was that Washington would pay our salaries, seventy-two dollars a month, and that Swaziland would provide transportation. Eventually, the four of us in small-business development received a pair of Suzuki 120 motorbikes. That meant I had to share mine with Jim Morphy, who'd been posted to another province — one hundred miles away.

My basic pattern of work was first to ride my Suzuki into a rural area, then enter the local trading store and ask for the owner. I would have him take a student's copybook down off the shelf, then begin teaching my stunned host, using my limited Zulu, how to keep a proper cash book.

As the weeks became months I got to know these fellows. A generation older than me, they could not have been nicer. Their main concern seemed to be my welfare. They would go out of their way to find a Coke for me when I turned up. They would fuss over their surprise visitor, this skinny young white guy from America.

Believe me: They treated me like a son. And while on the subject, I should note that during my entire two years in the country, 1968–1970, I never sensed a note of hostility from any Swazi. At a reception he gave for Peace Corps volunteers in the province, the new district commissioner greeted his guests by observing what an "adventure" it must be for us to come all the way to Africa.

I thought of myself as sort of a bourgeois Che Guevara. I was traveling around a Third World country preaching the ways of capitalism just as Che had been hawking Marxism in South America. If I wasn't in Vietnam, I was serving the cause on another front. While far less dangerous, it was also more promising.

In addition to my visiting road show I organized a number of weeklong business schools. I would recruit ten to twenty traders, arrange for their housing at a local boarding school, hire a smart young student to serve as interpreter, pull together a faculty of teachers, and get some movies from the United States Information Agency (USIA) as a treat to show in the evening. The courses included basic marketing techniques, such as lowering prices to increase total revenues.

I also set up a national industrial show. It was a fairly big affair staged on the national fairgrounds. Even the king came and liked it. So did the United Nations adviser who was assigned to small-business development.

After the mamba incident, my most unforgettable moment came at a meeting with seventeen Swazi guys. All of them were small traders, the people I'd come thousands of miles to teach. What I remember clearly is that I knew each of them as an individual, knew them decently well in fact. It struck me at the time that I was the only non-Swazi in the room, the only white guy. While there were volunteers who were far enemy, Barry Goldwater, and later Ronald Reagan, left it to the establishment to argue the war. The home-front conflict over Vietnam was fought within the Democratic party.

The only Republican voice heard in 1968, when the casualty rate was ten thousand soldiers a year, was that of Richard Nixon, who was promising a secret plan to extract us from the war. A strategy that would replicate the casualties of the Johnson presidency and give a Republican stamp to the war.

Had I come to Washington in 1961, I would have been a reasonably thoughtful conservative, one with some doubts about the shortcomings of the party ideology in the area of civil rights and Social Security. But when I actually arrived a decade later, I was ready to look for a job with a Democrat or, failing that, a moderate, antiwar Republican.

better at the language, even ones far more committed to their work, this was the one time when I fully grasped the essence of the Peace Corps. The adventure is not just the travel in a foreign country; it's the personal connection with the people living there.

Of course, the travel wasn't bad. I remember driving my Suzuki into Lourenco Marques one Friday night. I stopped for a great Portuguese dinner, including a carafe of white wine, at a roadside restaurant. Just an hour east of Swaziland, the old Mozambique was a port city of sidewalk cafés, modern movie theaters, bullfights, and men selling lottery tickets. I remember my long train ride through East Africa; the overnight run on the Rhodesian Railway from LM to Bulawayo, then hitchhiking alone from Rhodesia to Tanzania, and finally taking a twenty-six-hour ride on a local bus carrying chickens, goats, you name it, all the way to Kilimanjaro. I remember hitchhiking to Victoria Falls from the Zambian side, catching the incredible sight of it through the trees at sunset, then, in the darkness, crossing on foot the bridge that runs over the gorge just below the falls.

What were those two years like? I know just how to tell you. Working our way home in December 1970, three or four of us were in Mombasa seeing *The Wild Bunch* at a big downtown movie theater. It's the story of a tough old outlaw gang in the early years of the twentieth century. In the final scene, two survivors of the gang meet each other in a little Mexican town where one of them, played by Edmund O'Brien, has teamed up with the peasants to fight the *federales*. The Robert Ryan character asks him how it's going. "It ain't like it was," he answers, "but it'll do."

As we were walking down the street after the movie, Jim Steinman, a buddy of mine from California, repeated that line. Every one of us laughed at the happy truth of what he'd just said. For us it wasn't like it had been for the young British colonial officers who'd come out to work in countries like Swaziland. We didn't live quite the upscale life they had. We didn't have the cars and the clubs and the grand houses. But the positive side of the ledger was that, unlike those smart young Brits of yesteryear, we were working on the side of the people.

Like anyone who's been to the Peace Corps, I can never fully convey its impact on me. Grandmom-in-Chestnut-Hill shrewdly saw how I'd broken free on arrival back in the United States, after I'd gone down to Washington and started my climb on Capitol Hill. She spotted what had set me on a w[ ] different course from my four brothers. [ ] was Africa," she said, fixing me with [ ] stare, "wasn't it?"

Yes, Grandmom, I think it was.

HERE'S WHAT I REALLY THINK: The s[ ] ties changed me. If John F. Kennedy had n[ ] been assassinated, if the United States had n[ ] sent five hundred thousand troops in[ ] Vietnam, if I had not spent two years in th[ ] Peace Corps, my politics would be very di[ ] ferent today. For it is that combination of reali[ ] ties that cracked my conservative orthodoxy.

I still feel the death of JFK, a man who was far more conservative than his liberal legend, far tougher in life than the "Camelot" fantasy confected after his death. More than any other president, he had been growing in office. As my Republican dad once said, even as he prepared to vote for Nixon, you could hear a hint of Churchill in that young man.

Vietnam remains a chronic reminder that even the most powerful nation in the world cannot work its will everywhere. When the fight is on enemy turf, when the forces of nationalism are riding against you, beware!

And speaking of Vietnam, where were the American conservatives? Having pushed the hard line against the Communist

Chapter Seven

"The Worst Form of Government"

> Nobody pretends that democracy is perfect or all-wise. Indeed, it has been said that democracy is the worst form of Government except for all other forms that have been tried from time to time.
>
> Winston Churchill

I took my chair at MSNBC headquarters at 5:00 p.m. election night. At 5:00 a.m. the following morning I was still in that chair.

I'd known it was going to be tight. With three weeks left, I had predicted the 2000 presidential election would be a squeaker. I thought Gore would win points on the economy, Bush on his personality. "I think this election is going to be so close," I told Matt Lauer on that morning after the third debate, "that the Electoral College could go in the opposite direction of the popular vote."

139

What did I really think? To be perfectly honest, I thought it would go the other way, Gore winning the electoral vote, Bush winning the popular.

But who could have predicted that five-week overtime in Florida? I was on the air constantly and got an intimate look at the whole thing. Talk about political hardball! Everyone in that state had his or her hand in politics. We kept looking for a team of umpires to enter the arena, but all we ever got were more players. I could say that I'd never seen anything like it. But, as you've probably figured by now, it wouldn't be true. During three decades working in and around politicians, I've seen backroom scrounging for votes, officeholders fighting over jurisdictions, operatives using every lever they could to their advantage.

The five-week postelection fight over Florida, however, was unique in at least one regard: Whoever got the state's electoral votes would become president. For many Americans, just watching the ordeal on television was hardship duty. For me, it was both fascinating and the greatest professional opportunity of my life. In those thirty days I was able to exploit thirty years of experience in politics.

You know the insect life you expose when

you look under a rock? Aristophanes, the Greek playwright from the fourth century B.C., knew, "Under every stone lurks a politician." And that's exactly what many people saw when they stumbled upon the electoral anthropology of Florida last November. As someone who has spent years as a political bug, I found the terrain under that rock very familiar. Suddenly everyone, whatever their title, was a politician. From her first on-air appearance you could see that the secretary of state in St. John's knit was a Republican. Almost as quickly we learned that Florida's attorney general was a Democrat, while the people on the "canvassing boards" each had his or her own easy-to-spot allegiances. The Florida Supreme Court was packed with liberals picked by Democratic governors.

It was my joy — I have to use that word — to spend five weeks on MSNBC pointing out the inconvenient reality of how politics really works in this country. Not through made-for-TV speeches and rallies, but through real street fights, through skirmishing for votes block by block.

It all reminded me of a typical week on Capitol Hill. With the big vote set for Thursday night, the vote-scrounging would begin in earnest on Tuesday. General

141

debate would get underway on Wednesday. All the while, unofficial party "task forces" would be out in force, figuring out how to spring one more vote free from the other side. You would see jurisdictional disputes, fights over the rules, debates over procedures, the ongoing skirmishing for numbers, numbers, numbers.

My Washington education began for me when I came to town with two hundred dollars left of my post-Swaziland "readjustment allowance." My strategy was simple: Get a job with a senator or member of Congress and work my way up the political ladder. My dream was to be a legislative assistant to a senator, because that was the job Ted Sorensen had performed for John F. Kennedy. His memoir of those early years was a book I had devoured eagerly while serving in the Peace Corps; it was my companion one particular night on a long overnight train ride from Mozambique to Rhodesia.

So I went up to Capitol Hill and started knocking on doors, introducing myself to perfect strangers much as I had done with Swazi traders during the previous two years. Fortunately, it worked. Wayne Owens, then a top aide to Senator Frank Moss of Utah, loved the fact that I'd just come from the

Peace Corps and hired me, though not before he made me try out. He asked me to write a response tò a very difficult letter from a woman who was very influential in cultural circles in Salt Lake City. She wanted to know if her husband was eligible for a tax shelter for people who work in non-profit organizations. I went over to the IRS and sat down with a tax expert. I typed up everything he gave me, did a number of revisions, then walked into the senator's office Monday morning with the product.

I remember standing there waiting for Wayne's verdict. He read it, liked it, and said, "I'm going to give you a job as a Capitol policeman. I know that's not what you had hoped for, but it will pay for the groceries."

I took it.

My heart in my stomach, I said it wasn't what I had hoped for but I was grateful, and, of course, ready to go to work. The drill was, I would work daytimes in the office answering complicated letters from constituents and writing short speeches. At 3:00, I'd don my uniform and .38 special and take up my guard duties. One evening I was posted outside a backroom in the Capitol and told to let no one past. I was protecting the "Pentagon papers."

By summer's end I had pestered Wayne into making me a legislative assistant to the senator. I drafted speeches and suggested amendments to pending bills. I also began to learn some potent insider lessons about politics.

One was "patronage." I found out that to get any job on Capitol Hill you needed a senator or member of Congress to appoint you.

I also began to grasp the truth of that old Hemingway adage, "Don't confuse action with movement." I discovered that the signature you get on a letter from a senator saying how he's working diligently on the matter you raised in a letter is probably the penmanship of a state-of-the-art signature machine. I learned that a bill passed in one body of Congress may be predestined to go nowhere in the other. (In fact, amendments are often allowed precisely because the chief counsel of the committee of jurisdiction knows they're going nowhere.) I saw sixty-five senators grab a bit of positive publicity by passing an "ironclad" ceiling on federal spending only to, hours later, jam past a pair of amendments rendering it useless. I saw senators defeat a bill indexing the minimum wage to inflation and productivity so that they — I'm talking about the Democrats —

could keep their good buddies in the labor unions dependent on their good graces.

These are valuable things to learn when you're just starting out.

After two years with Senator Moss, I got some encouragement from him that I have never forgotten: "Chris, maybe you ought to dip a little deeper in the political waters." So, in December 1972, following Nixon's big re-election, I wrote a long piece for the old *Washington Star* headlined, "An Issue Democrats Ignore at their Peril." That issue was fiscal responsibility. Either the Democrats should kick their deficit-spending habit, I wrote, or they would never be taken seriously. Four years later Jimmy Carter would win the party's presidential nomination with a promise to make government more efficient. It would take Bill Clinton, though, to show voters that the Democrats meant business.

In spring 1974, I decided to follow Senator Moss's advice and challenge the incumbent — and the Democratic machine — in a Philadelphia congressional primary. I had no money, no big-name support, no small-name support, no plan. It was quixotic and exhilarating. I remember that the guy who volunteered to do my printing wrote me in a letter: "Matthews, you've got steel balls."

My first step was to get myself registered to vote locally; the next was to file as a candidate. I went down to City Hall and found out how many signatures I needed for the petition. Then I went out and started walking along my old paper route, down Southampton road to Londontown, collecting names. My campaign consisted of visiting high schools, asking kids to volunteer, then assigning them areas where they would distribute my literature.

The "Matthews for Congress" campaign did wild things, such as having a volunteer rock band play to drum up crowds at shopping centers. My favorite gambit was to have a crowd of volunteers, which included a number of very cute Catholic high-school girls, stand alongside the district's main traffic artery, Roosevelt Boulevard, waving "Honk 'n' Wave" signs. We had four hundred kids signed up.

I told my volunteers that I was running against the corruption revealed by the Watergate probe, the fat cat campaign gifts aimed at controlling the men in office. I told them I had nobody giving me money — that was certainly true — and that, therefore, they were my fat cats. My kids were "good government" through and through, and if any of those great people are now reading this, I want you to know how grateful I am to this day.

Beaten badly on primary day, I nonetheless gained new stature back in Washington. Senator Moss got his friend Edmund Muskie of Maine to hire me to work for the new Senate Budget Committee. Muskie had been a big reason I'd voted for Humphrey in '68. He had run for president in '72 but lost the nomination to George McGovern. But in the Senate he was the one man with the guts to make Congress design a budget every year and stick to it, just like a family has to. I remember Hubert Humphrey — he was a big spender and knew it — passing Muskie, his friend and colleague, in the Senate chambers and telling him, "You're doing great stuff, Ed. I couldn't do it."

Ed Muskie was the senator who passed the Clean Water and Air Acts on the budget committee. I saw how he got things done. While other senators would come, get their pictures taken, give short speeches, and leave, he would just sit there and work. He would not even go to the bathroom. We on his staff used to call him "Iron Butt." Because of that, he became a very productive legislator; while other members came and went, he stayed and legislated.

You might say Senator Muskie was practical to a fault. I remember saying to him, after working for three years on the budget committee, "You know, if we had a parliamentary system in this country, you would be prime minister." His response to my tribute was blunt: "But we don't, do we?" That was Muskie. It took a lawmaker that stoic to spend all those years telling senators to spend only what they were willing to tax.

During my years on Capitol Hill, I was always working on my speechwriting and public-speaking skills. I accepted every speaking opportunity regardless of the group: the Close-Up Foundation, Presidential Classroom, the Brookings Institution. I joined the Capitol Hill chapter of Toastmasters. While other staffers were content just knowing their stuff, I forced myself to practice getting that stuff across to other people. I desperately needed to overcome my stage fright.

In 1977, former Florida speaker of the house Dick Pettigrew hired me to work in the White House on President Carter's number-one campaign promise: government reorganization. Two years later, chief presidential speechwriter Hendrik Hertzberg hired me to join his team. Of all the jobs I've had until *Hardball*, being a presidential speechwriter was the most fun.

At the time, Kathy and I were dating and heading toward marriage. Rik and I and the other speechwriters would work into the night, then Kathy would join us for late dinners.

My best Carter speechwriting memories, ironically, are of the failed reelection campaign. I was on board Air Force One during that last exhausting week, when in one Saturday President Carter stopped at five different Texas cities, and then headed to Milwaukee and Chicago. We got to bed at about two in the morning only to be awakened two hours later with the word that the Iranian parliament had voted on what might be acceptable conditions for the release of our fifty hostages. On the way back to Washington, those of us bumped to the second plane were gleeful and starting to plan the second term. We assumed that the hostages were going to come home before the election and that Jimmy Carter actually was going to pull what the Republicans were calling his "October Surprise."

It didn't turn out that way. The Iranian conditions were still unreasonable, and the impression the voters got was that President Carter had been humiliated. When defeat came in an election-eve call from pollster

Patrick Caddell, we on the staff endured it together. My departure from the White House took place at twenty minutes to noon on Ronald Reagan's Inaugural day.

Opportunity would knock again soon. Early in 1981, Martin Franks, a young researcher at the Democratic National Committee, was named executive director of the Democratic Congressional Campaign Committee. He and his boss, California congressman Tony Coelho, hired me to work for them behind the scenes with House Speaker Thomas P. "Tip" O'Neill, Jr., the last Democratic leader to survive the Reagan landslide.

Within a few months, Tip's administrative assistant resigned and the Speaker named me as his replacement. It had taken me a decade to rise from Capitol policeman to the top staff position on Capitol Hill. Administrative assistant to the Speaker: It was to be the greatest — and toughest — public service experience of my life so far. For the next six years I worked for a man who was a mountain of courage, history, and goodwill.

When the tension between President Reagan and Speaker O'Neill began to grow, I was one of those urging him to stand and challenge the White House. I think he liked that. Somewhere in his heart, he already had decided to fight. "I like the way you carry yourself," he said, as a way to explain the trust he had placed in me.

Tip O'Neill was who he was long before I got there. All I did was convince him that he could go on television and say the things that he felt out loud. My job was to construct a counterpulpit to the one in the White House. It turned out to be a wonderful tonic for Tip. I think he really enjoyed it, although he would much rather have spent those golden years as top kick to an activist Democratic president.

Nothing gives me a better feeling about the Hill than my memory from those six years with Tip of a Republican congressman crossing the floor to ask a Democrat he'd been debating what he had planned for the weekend and to say hello to his wife. That is the civil republic our Founding Fathers must have imagined all those years ago in my hometown of Philadelphia.

I respect men and women who take the risk to run for Congress. It takes guts. It's all pass/fail. And it's personal. You lose and you're a loser. Your friends feel sorry for you and for the rest of your family. "Oh, they should have elected you," people keep saying to you when you're alone. It's always there in your heart. It never goes away.

Anyone who risks that kind of public rejection deserves respect.

And to those turned off by the fighting and shouting on Capitol Hill, let me offer a warning: The day we stop fighting, prepare yourselves for a new and dangerous form of government in this country. Democracy is, by nature, noisy. And as we saw in Florida, it doesn't always work so well.

By 1992 I had been writing a syndicated column for the *San Francisco Examiner* for four years. To make my point, in a piece I wrote mocking the pathetic voter turnout in the spring primaries that had nominated Bill Clinton for president, I noted that just 15 percent of the adults in Michigan had bothered to vote on March 17. That was the same percentage of South Africa's adult population that had voted in their national elections that same day. But in South Africa at that time only the whites were permitted to vote.

Swaziland, the country where I had served in the Peace Corps, was bordered by South Africa on three sides. As American volunteers living there, we were never allowed to cross that border. The apartheid government did not want men and women like us contaminating its society with our liberal attitudes on race relations. Within a few days of my arrival, in fact, a commentator on the SABC, the South African Broadcasting Corporation, attacked our contingent in Swaziland as "do-gooding intellectuals." In a menacing tone he added that an earlier Peace Corps group had been kicked out of the country for getting involved in local politics. The truth was, the British had just given Swaziland its independence that September 1968. We were the first Peace Corps group to ever enter the country.

I believe that you only really pay attention to what you discover for yourself. Before coming to the subcontinent, my feelings toward South Africa were the usual mix. I knew that racial supremacy was wrong. At the same time, I couldn't help but marvel at the spunk of those tough Afrikaner farmers who had built up the country and held out against the British in the Boer War.

However, one's attitude quickly changes when one becomes, even in the slightest way, a marked enemy of such a country. For the entire two years we were nestled just across the border and denied entry to the nation that virtually surrounded us. The U.S. government did nothing in protest, no doubt fearing, correctly, that some of our group might cause trouble if forced to comply with the apartheid rules.

We couldn't cross the border, but many South Africans came to Swaziland. Desperate for a ride, I once boarded one of the big South African buses that would occasionally lumber through the southern part of the country where I taught business to the local traders. The driver insisted that I take a seat in a small compartment up front. "No Europeans in the back," he said, as he moved some cargo so I could have space to sit. I also got a good taste of the South African mentality watching the young white men arriving to spend drunken weekends with the Swazi bar girls. Many of my impressions of South Africa came from listening to the SABC on my shortwave radio and reading the *Rand Daily Mail*, which managed daily the feat of juxtaposing triumphs like Christiaan Barnard's miraculous heart transplants with less upbeat matters such as the relentless enforcement of "immorality laws" banning sexual contact between whites and blacks.

My first glimpse of life within South Africa was the night my fellow volunteer Steve Hank and I spent in Johannesburg on the way home. Both film buffs, we went to see the movie *Woodstock*. What I didn't realize until later was how much of the film had been edited for local consumption. What I did experience right away was the creepy feeling you get living as a white in a country where every day blacks have fresh reasons for hating you. You don't know how horrible it is to go into a restaurant where only whites can go and to be served by black waiters until you've done it.

Twelve years later, I returned to Swaziland with my wife, Kathy. We were on a three-country tour of Africa with the United States Information Agency, giving lectures about how the media works in a free society. Back in the country where I had spent two years and had felt at home, I was stunned to confront for the first time local hostility toward America. The Swazi people with whom I had lived and worked had nothing bad to say about the United States — ever. The fact was that Swaziland was not a very political country from 1968 to 1971.

What a difference a decade had made! Meeting with some students at the university, I saw how much our country's support for South Africa was costing us. Some of the young people were spouting the predictable Marxist line on U.S. foreign policy, and they had all the talking points.

"The first successful move against imperialism took place in 1917," said one especially militant student from the back of the lecture hall. "The whole of U.S. policy in Africa is dictated by economics."

My attempts to explain that there was opposition to the Reagan administration's policy of "constructive engagement" with South Africa did no good. Afterward, when I asked the instructor to explain this particularly aggressive student's story, he told me, "He was in jail for a year in South Africa."

In 1985 I caught another inside glimpse into South African racial politics when U.S. congressman Bill Gray, a fellow Philadelphian, asked me to join a congressional delegation to the country. There was one stop on the trip that I will never forget nor fully comprehend. President P. W. Botha, the last of the die-hard Afrikaners, received us at his Indian Ocean retreat, known as the Wilderness. Located halfway between Cape Town and Port Elizabeth, it is a spectacular spot tucked between the mountains and the Indian Ocean. A sunny outpost of palm trees, red-bloomed hibiscus, and clean Dutch architecture, the peaks of the Great Karoo Mountains rising above and the deep blue sea beyond, the scene is direct from an artist's easel.

And there we were — a U.S. delegation

composed mostly of African-American congressmen, meeting in a seaside paradise re-
served for whites. I think Botha had the idea
that I, as a top aide to the Speaker of the
U.S. House of Representatives, was along
to keep watch over our largely African-
American group. He admonished his guests
not to expect change overnight. Any re-
forms would have to be sold to the white
voters. After all, he said, South Africa is a
"democracy."

Even more bizarre was the backdrop to
the conference. Throughout the entire late-
morning meeting I could hear the noises of
white vacationing families waiting in line at
the snack bar outside. It could have been
the lunchtime scene at Ocean City, New
Jersey, with kids and parents waiting for
their hot dogs and hamburgers.

For the visiting American congressmen,
lunch would be completely different.

After President Botha ended the morning
meeting, we moved to a room upstairs.
There we were greeted by a gigantic dining
table attended by a cadre of black waiters
each in a paisley costume and fez. For two
hours we were treated to food, wine, and
service redolent of the raj.

By year's end, the U.S. Congress had
passed the Comprehensive Anti-Apartheid

Act over Ronald Reagan's veto, slamming tough sanctions on South Africa. I favored the decision to cut off all U.S. investment, not in hope of smothering the South African economy but in hope that it would wake up the white government to reality. I may have been right. In 1989, a bitter and frustrated Botha suffered a stroke and was forced to retire by the young members of his Nationalist party who were ready to bite the bullet. Their leader was the visionary F. W. de Klerk, who replaced Botha and quickly legalized the African National Congress. He also released Nelson Mandela from his twenty-eight years of imprisonment and this prepared his country for democratic rule.

In 1994, ABC's *Good Morning America* sent me to South Africa to cover the very first all-races election. I had won the assignment by convincing *GMA* executive producer Bob Reichblum that the language and cross-cultural skills I'd gained in Swaziland a generation before would make me the perfect correspondent.

When the ABC producers and I arrived in Johannesburg on the eve of the election, the white diehards had begun their bombing campaign. They started by detonating a bomb right outside the ANC headquarters. It didn't work. "Although they are scared," local reporter Rich Mkhondo told me, "the bombing is actually encouraging people to vote."

"I'll be damned if the bombers are going to keep me from voting," one woman told me.

A quarter-century ago, the world had just thirty democracies. Daniel Patrick Moynihan, then the U.S. ambassador to the United Nations, viewed their future with pessimism: "Democracy is beginning to look like monarchy. It is the place where the world was, not where it is going. So America is not what countries are going to be like. For the rest of our natural lives we will be in a world in which there are very few of us and a great many of them."

Fortunately, this was that rare occasion where the great Pat Moynihan turned out to be wrong. The world begins the twenty-first century with 120 democracies, including many with little or no history of self-government. South Africa, Bangladesh, Poland, the Czech Republic, Greece, Spain, Portugal, Taiwan, South Korea, and many others all enjoy freedom of speech, the right to hold public meetings, and an independent media. Compare this to the 1970s, when even free multiparty elections were a rarity outside of Europe and North America.

HERE'S WHAT I REALLY THINK: I think democracy is the only way to keep a check on governmental power. You have to be able to turn the bums out from time to time. I think the United States should continue to share that hard-earned lesson. The more countries that hold elections, the fewer dictatorships the world will have to endure. The more true self-government, the more of the world's people who will benefit from basic human rights. And countries with true freedom of expression, true freedom of religion, are generally inhospitable to warmongers. One of the highlights of 2001 was the decision at the Summit of the Americas in Quebec to limit participation to countries committed to free elections. As my friends in South Africa understood all too well, "Democracy is the worst form of government except for all the others that have been tried from time to time."

TIP O'NEILL

The voice on the phone was familiar, and it was angry, "I don't mind you making a fool out of yourself, but you're not going to make one out of me!" It was Thomas P. "Tip" O'Neill, Jr., the famous Democratic Speaker of the House I served during his six-year ideological brawl with Republican president Ronald Reagan. Two years into retirement his full-throttle partisan rage had locked onto a new target: me.

How in the world, he demanded to know, could I have said on *CBS This Morning* the previous day that Dan Quayle had earned more points than Lloyd Bentsen in the vice-presidential debate? Everybody knew Bentsen, the senior senator from Texas, had killed the young Indiana senator. What was I up to, saying such a ridiculous thing? What kind of game was I playing?

From the rough tone in his voice and the unusually early hour — it was barely eight on a Saturday morning — I quickly deduced what had happened. My old boss had just endured an entire night of gin rummy, with pals giving him relentless grief for the idiotic verdict "his guy" had delivered that morning.

If it had been anybody other than Tip I would have lined up my excuses. I had been honestly impressed with Quayle's appearance. But I must have been crazy to score the debate on points when the only exchange anyone remembered was Bentsen's roundhouse punch that came after Quayle had dared compare his own position in Congress to that of another senator running for national office back in 1960.

"I knew Jack Kennedy. I worked with Jack Kennedy. Jack Kennedy was my friend. Senator, you're no Jack Kennedy," Bentsen had sneered. I was a fool not to know that the networks would replay it again and again over the following days. Realizing that he had made his point, and remembering that it always was a mismatch between us, Tip ended his early-morning assault, switching his giant voice from growl to gruff: "How's Kathy? What's up with the family? Talk to you later."

I was lucky to know and serve Tip O'Neill in what many felt was his finest hour as a Democrat, or more important, as an American leader. I don't claim to be objective. I was there when the big, white-haired guy from the street corners of North Cambridge stood alone, reminding us all that when we ask God to bless America, we are not praying just for the young, the healthy, and the rich. When people ask me what it was like working for Tip O'Neill, and about the man himself, I think of a moment that has nothing to do with Democrats or Republicans, liberals or conservatives, or with politics at all — except in the most personal sense of the word.

It was a snowy afternoon in March 1982. We were sitting, the Speaker and I, in one of those miniature Lear jets that corporate executives use to zip about the country. But the weather was anything but zippy. Through the window I could see the snow piling deep on the National Airport runway, the wheels of the landing gear beginning to disappear, the glass on the windows starting to freeze, the image of the Air Florida disaster throbbing in my head. Just weeks before a plane taking off from this same airport with too much ice on its wings had never cleared the Potomac. That thought was with me when I caught the eye of the giant figure sitting in the plane's backmost seat. I wondered what perversity of chance-taking had led him to take the seat farthest to the rear, making it all the more difficult for the little plane to get up off the snow.

"What are you worrying about?" issued from the face beneath the Irish tweed walking hat. I thought but didn't say: "We're about to fly this midget plane out into God knows what. Even if we're lucky enough to take off, we could end up slipping through the ice of Lake Erie, never to be seen again!" And why were we taking this little out-and-back jaunt anyway? Because some freshman congressman from a working-class district near Detroit had asked Tip to speak for him, to liven up a couple of afternoon fund-raisers that nobody back in Washington would ever hear of or care about — unless we didn't make it back.

Really, what was I worrying about?

Some questions have no reasonable, much less polite, answers, especially when they come from the boss. Mumbling something about the "weather," I tried to forget the powerful presence before me as I returned to the white-knuckled hell of that frost-covered porthole.

What was Tip O'Neill like to work for? That's what he was like. I'm not saying he didn't worry — he just didn't let people see him do it, even as he was taking his "all politics is local" brand of leadership up into a little plane and doing battle with the gale

164

force reality of early 1980s Reaganism.

Let's not forget the circumstances back then. A conservative president had just come to town. Jimmy Carter was banished back to Georgia, his party routed. Ronald Reagan was charming the country with his affability while claiming a mandate for big Pentagon budgets and "supply-side" economic policies at home. Liberals, the few who still admitted to the label, sulked in bitter, humiliated silence. Except for one hulking white-haired guy who refused to quit.

I can remember exactly when the fight started between him and Reagan. It was an afternoon in June 1981. For months, the Speaker had been getting himself used to the idea that he'd become more than Speaker of the House: He was the country's last standing Democrat. The Republicans had the White House. They had the Senate. Only the House blocked the Reagan Revolution's victory parade. Only the Speaker had the stature and the pulpit to challenge the popular president's policies. But it was not until that particular June afternoon that the full reality of Tip O'Neill's late-career role would become crystal clear to him, to Reagan and to the country.

A crowd of us was sitting in the Speaker's

office when the decision was made. The president had just said at a nationally televised press conference that the Speaker of the House was guilty of "sheer demagoguery" for questioning the fairness of his program.

It was ABC-TV's agent provocateur, Sam Donaldson, who had lit the match.

"Tip O'Neill says you don't know anything about the working people, that you have just a bunch of wealthy and selfish advisers," he said to the president, as Reagan headed for the door.

That ignited it. Suddenly the debonair Reagan returned to the microphones. "I think it's sheer demagoguery," he said, "to pretend that this economic program is not aimed at helping the great cross-section of people."

"Demagoguery!" As the news wires raced with the president's attack and the evening news programs prepared their stories, the target stood in his office, deciding how to handle it. He listened to the arguments for letting Reagan's remark pass and to those who urged a partisan counterpunch. As always, the big man from Massachusetts went with his instincts. "I'm going up to the gallery," he said. At that, he went into the bathroom, combed his hair, and straightened his tie. He then left the sanctuary of the Speaker's office behind, took the elevator to the Capitol's third floor, walked into the radio-TV gallery, and said what he, as the Speaker of the House, thought of what he had just seen and heard on television.

What he said to the network cameras was not really about the party. Instead he focused on the relationship between his job and Ronald Reagan's. After all, he was the elected Speaker of the House of Representatives and that office deserved a certain respect from the head of another branch of government. He was there now to insist on that respect.

While nonpartisan in substance, O'Neill's rejoinder could not have been more partisan in effect. By challenging Reagan's offhand comment about "demagoguery," he was hitting the new president where he was the weakest, in his appreciation of governmental institutions. He said that he, the Speaker of the House, would never accuse a president of the United States of being a "demagogue." "I assume in the future," O'Neill said, that the president would show "the same respect for the speakership." Then he brought out his big guns. "The Reagan program speaks for itself," he told the cameras that tense afternoon. "It is geared to the wealthy."

Just as Tip O'Neill had heard the fighting words in Reagan's remark about "sheer demagoguery," the other man felt the return fire. A few minutes after O'Neill's words about the new kid on the block lacking respect for the speakership, Reagan was on the phone with him, pleading for peace, and soon the White House staff had an announcement to make: What the president had said did not reflect on the Speaker.

Right.

That's how it all started. Reagan had taken a swing at Tip O'Neill. When the day ended, the Speaker was not only still standing, but taller than ever. He, the country's top-ranking Democrat, had questioned not just the cuts in Social Security and student loans but the partisan motives that drove them. He had stood up to Ronald Reagan one June afternoon in 1981 and the other guy had blinked.

The real Reagan-O'Neill fight was over policy, not protocol. Reagan saw Social Security cuts as a budget savings. Tip saw them as a wound inflicted on the working family that depends clearly on its monthly check. Reagan saw the double-digit jobless rates of his first term as a necessary damper on inflation. Speaker O'Neill saw the faces of the unemployed in those rising numbers.

Waging almost nightly war on the evening news, as he came to do, was not Tip O'Neill's natural field of combat. He was a backroom pol and proud of it. He was a street corner guy who made his friends and deals one at a time, face-to-face. When it came to press relations, he preferred dealing with print guys he had known for years. He liked the familiar, ink-stained old world of friends you trusted and enemies you didn't, where you talked to some reporters and stiffed the others. He never got used to the world of independent (and therefore unpredictable) journalists who, depending on the circumstances, would as easily praise as demolish you.

I used to have to beg him to do interviews, and each time I did risk it my butt was on the line. He always assumed that the reporter was a pal of mine. Why else would I so willingly risk the boss's wrath? I desperately wanted to tell him that I had let the reporter in because my job was to help him become what he could become, and the way to do that was to be publicized. And the only way to be publicized was to let people write about him. And the only way to let them write about him was to let them take some shots at him.

That is the only way to become a figure in American politics. You cannot customize it. You cannot come in and tailor it. All you can do is go in, allow reporters to see who you are, and let them make their own judgments about you. It's a distillation, not an accumulation. You can have twenty brickbats thrown at you, and what matters is what comes through.

Tip made the adjustment — and at a time in life when most men are past retirement. "An old dog can learn new tricks," he said to me one day in his office, and that's just what he did. The fellow who had won the speakership of the Massachusetts House of Representatives, election to Congress seventeen times, election to the U.S. speakership five times by going one-on-one with people, adjusted himself to the camera, the lights, and even to the makeup.

And what came across was what he was: a big guy with a good heart and a lot of guts.

The late Kirk O'Donnell, Tip's counsel and political strategist, was always there with me. He was, to use the Speaker's own fond and proud salute, "hard as a rock." In a world of scaredy-cats and bullshitters, Kirk was a man of courage and heart, especially for the big fight.

I learned a lot of old-style politics working for Tip O'Neill: how to get a meeting over with by keeping the door closed, the thermostat up, and the cigar lit; how to settle a fight in that crowded room by blasting the guy you actually agree with (it makes those on the other side feel good, even if they don't get their way). But I also learned that to win an ongoing battle you need two things: guts and something to believe in. At a time when many in his party were buckling to Reagan's popularity, he kept his values. At a time when his fellow Democrats checked the weather reports before flying, he went anywhere a friend needed help. He was a leader with the nerve to fly into the most treacherous winds with only his prayers and principles to carry him.

For me, part of the fun of working for Tip O'Neill was to catch that Irishness of his. It often came as a surprise, with an odd remark, like his reference to the U.S. Senate as being the "home to the idiot sons of the rich." Or when he said that the wealthy would have to "pay through the nose" for a new Reagan defense proposal. Hearing him come out with a comment like that would have Kirk and me sweating for hours. But such over-the-top candor is also what made the Speaker's daily press conferences not only a delight to attend, but dangerous for a reporter to skip.

Tip O'Neill knew who he was. "That's not me," he said when I drafted a statement attacking Reagan's big deficits. He knew he wasn't a budget balancer and he wasn't going to pretend. His finest lesson to all political gladiators both of Left and Right is that one doesn't always get to pick one's ground. Tip would have much preferred to serve as Speaker under an activist, liberal, Democratic president like Walter Mondale. He would have loved to get bills through to help more poor kids go to college, gotten health protection for working families, put more people to work. But that role wasn't in the cards he was dealt. It was his fate to be the one raising the banner of "fairness" in the face of a very popular conservative president. I doubt that anyone could have done a better job. Then again, I can't think of anyone less objective than myself to make that judgment.

In the years after Tip's retirement from the speakership I would call him up for lunch and we'd go to his favorite table at the Palm. As always, it was a thrill to be with him, as one of his pals. I remember our last lunch. He was having trouble walking and asked to lean on my shoulder as we walked the few short blocks. We were talking about the upcoming Boston College game with Notre Dame. He didn't think they'd be able to pull a second upset in two years. (They did!) It was during one of those last lunches that he told me the story of what a young flight attendant had recently said to him. He had just gotten on the plane and she was asking him to buckle up. As she assisted him with his belt, she said, "I hear that somebody important will be on this flight."

He looked at me squarely across the table and said, "Chris, it goes away."

At this year's White House Correspondents Association black-tie dinner some guy who'd apparently had too much to drink yelled out to me that "Tip O'Neill is spinning in his grave." He kept saying it, all the time with the dull stare of a car bomber on his face. He was referring, it can be assumed, to my failure to back the Democratic party line.

My response? I did not go into political journalism and commentary to speak for my old Democratic boss any more than I went into politics to speak for my Republican parents. I think, write, and speak for myself. People need to know, and they should, that what they get from me is, right or wrong, left or right, entirely and completely me.

What would Tip O'Neill have said about Clinton's conduct? I would bet he'd have played the good soldier. He would have pointed to the jobs created on his watch, the stronger economy, the greater opportunities for working families. And in regard to the desecration of the Oval Office, I think Tip would have probably expressed his sympathy for Mrs. Clinton and the president's daughter, Chelsea. But he would have been biting his tongue. Anyone who believes Tip O'Neill would have condoned Clinton's behavior didn't know the man and doesn't appreciate his legacy.

What would Tip think about some of the other things I say on *Hardball* or write in my column? One thing you can bet on is that he would have let me know, most likely early in the morning.

Of course, the most famous image of my old boss may be the one from when he appeared on *Cheers*. He and George Wendt are sitting at the end of the bar with mugs in hand. I like the scene because it shows how a politician, if he's true to his principles and roots, can become something of a folk hero.

That young stewardess was right.

CHAPTER EIGHT

TRUTH

DON'T BE AFRAID TO SEE WHAT YOU SEE.
RONALD REAGAN

The truth hurts. I think the hardest and best reporting occurs when you come back with the story that is neither expected nor well-received. Usually, those stories are ones that deal with subjects both vital to our society and deeply divisive.

Race relations is surely the most important of such areas. Myself, I don't trust what people tell pollsters about race. I think it's one topic that is immune to public candor.

For example, polls often fail to stop the resistance of white voters to black candidates for office. When he ran for California governor, Los Angeles mayor Tom Bradley got better numbers from polled voters than he did in the actual balloting. So did former Virginia governor Douglas Wilder, a man whose apparent double-digit edge practically evaporated on election day.

Ever wonder why this country has no black U.S. senators, no black governors? I've spoken to hundreds of Fortune 500 corporations and national trade associations over the years and enjoyed their company. Would someone tell me why these conventions and meetings have so few African Americans?

Race, without question, is the San Andreas Fault in American society. Folks are just plain afraid to be straightforward about the situation for fear that the answers will be used against them.

I say we'd be better off if we admitted out differences. We'll also be better off when white people open their hearts to voting for black people for higher office and when the Republicans once again contest the Democrats for black votes. Richard Nixon got about a third of the black vote in 1960; George W. Bush got about 3 percent in 2000.

A poll taken by *The Washington Post* in 2001 shows that most white people believe that blacks have it as good in this country as they do. Seven out of ten white people agreed with the statement: "African Americans have more or about the same opportunities in life as whites have." This reminds me of another poll that showed just one African American in three believing that O. J. Simpson killed his ex-wife, Nicole. In both cases, pollsters are posing questions of fact and getting back answers of *attitude*.

Ever watch an NBA game and notice that the players are mostly black but nearly 100 percent of the seats within one hundred feet of the court are filled with whites? Ever go anywhere and not see the whites in the better seats, the better houses, the better jobs?

It reminds me of the Groucho Marx line, "Are you going to believe me or your lying eyes?" I ask you to look behind that *Washington Post* poll measuring white perceptions of black opportunity. The truth is, white people know there's discrimination in this country: they just prefer not to admit it, a luxury denied to those regularly experiencing discrimination. I believe they refuse to acknowledge it for the same reason that blacks refuse to admit O.J. killed Nicole: It wouldn't look good.

There is no doubt that affirmative action is an important tool to use in correcting the continuing fallout of our racial past. With regard to "reparations," an idea that waxes and wanes, I believe what Abraham Lincoln said in his Second Inaugural Address, that the price for slavery was paid in full with the blood of those six hundred thousand men killed in the Civil War.

Science

Vice-President Dick Cheney urged America in 2001 to kill the loose talk about alternative energy sources. We should accept as an enduring fact of life that if we want heat, light, or to move something, the real options are oil, gas, coal, or nuclear.

Just two days later top Senate Democrat Tom Daschle took the same defeatist line against missile defense. We should accept as an enduring fact of life that if Russia or China or Iraq ever lobs an ICBM our way, he implied, the best we can do is lob one back.

Both positions were based not on science but on partisan ideology.

The Right — and Dick Cheney is clearly a man of the Right — has no real problem with a society dependent on extracting fossil fuel as fast as our SUVs can guzzle it. He regards the traffic jam heading for the nearest shopping mall as no more than the joyous clog of commerce.

The Left, for reasons I find hard to

fathom, takes the same unthoughtful approach toward efforts to develop an American defense against nuclear missiles. Such thinking is especially out of character for the Democratic party. After all, it was FDR who rammed through the Manhattan Project in time to end World War II without costing this country a million lives on the beaches of Japan. It was Jack Kennedy who launched the Apollo program that put a man on the moon in 1969, several years ahead of JFK's original schedule.

"I don't know how you support the deployment of a program that doesn't work," Daschle said of missile defense. But what both he and Cheney are really saying is that they can live with the world we have. Democrat Daschle is comfortable relying on a global web of arms control protocols. Cheney, an oilman out of Wyoming, is comfortable in a world dependent on fossil fuels.

What makes both issues so worthy of serious debate is that we need a better, cleaner, safer world. The one we have needs fixing, and defending the status quo isn't the way to accomplish that.

We rightly mistrust the sight of politicians telling us what *cannot* be done in realms where they are far from expert. Let's get *real*. Just as politics is beyond the competence of most professors, so is science beyond the competence of most politicians.

Abortion Rights

In 1976, Senator-elect Daniel Patrick Moynihan warned that we would one day argue more over values than over economics. "If the day comes when we don't have the economic problem and all we can think about is religion, you may long for the age of the general strike. You can compromise on wages. There are moral issues that do not allow compromise and accommodation, and those can be hugely divisive."

Though we still debate tax cuts, the fight over values is growing more ferocious each year. In the abortion rights debate, despite the heat it continues to generate, there is never any genuine dialog. One of the reasons is that each side has become so insulated that it only speaks in its own vocabulary.

People on one side refuse even to speak the word abortion. Instead, they talk about "choice." Are we talking Pepsi or Coke? In a further burst of fuzziness, they speak of "reproductive" rights. Who are they kidding? Has anyone talked of stopping people from reproducing? If you want to protect abortion rights, you shouldn't be afraid of saying so. If you don't even like using the phrase "abortion rights," I only ask that you consider why.

On the other side, we find a different kind of linguistic disconnect. If you believe abortion is "murder," then what should be the punishment for the woman who seeks one? Life imprisonment? Ten years? Ten minutes?

The fact is — and it *is* a fact — the American people will not exact a token of punishment from a woman who seeks an abortion. Shouldn't this tell opponents of abortion rights something very basic? It tells me that the criminal code is not the right instrument here. We shouldn't be trying to use it for the basic reason that even most of those Americans who count themselves "pro-life" don't see going to get an abortion as a crime.

Shouldn't these basic semantic difficulties tell you something? Advocates are wary of saying the word "abortion" while opponents use the word "murder" but are wary of calling it a crime. In both cases, what actually points the way toward common ground are the messages behind the language.

I think the only way to reduce the number of abortions in the country dramatically is for the opponents of abortion rights to find common ground with those who think the final decision over abortion should remain constitutionally protected.

There are other ways to cut down on the number of abortions without outlawing them. And since abortion is not going to be outlawed, those other ways are the only ways we have.

I remember Clinton promising to make abortion "safe, legal, and rare." Still needed is a president who will make — and keep — such a promise.

Gay Rights

Anyone who defends job discrimination against gays should ask himself: If you don't let gay men and women provide for themselves, who should do it for them? Those who oppose civil unions among gay people should ask themselves: Aren't we better off having gay people involved in strong, enduring, recognized relationships than the alternative?

I give Bill Clinton credit here. He is the first president in history to openly acknowledge gay people as part of the American family. Just by showing up in 1997 at the national meeting of the Human Rights Campaign, the country's premier gay and lesbian rights organization, he made a lot of Americans feel very good about themselves. And I think Vice-President Cheney, whose daughter is openly gay, would publicly agree with that objective.

I once spoke to the annual dinner of the Log Cabin Club, a national organization of gay Republicans. The men I met that evening were proud, committed members of the GOP — and the GOP should be proud to have them.

The Gender Gap

Fifty-one percent of men voted for George W. Bush in the last election, just 43 percent for Albert Gore. Fifty percent of women voted for Gore, just 43 percent for Bush. I have an explanation for this breakdown. It has to do with interests.

First, let me identify those interests. Ask a man what shots his kids have had. What are their teachers' names? Who telephones the grandparents more often? He or his wife? Second, who goes around the house at night obsessively turning out lights? Who goes downstairs to check when someone hears a floor creak?

The answers go a long way toward explaining why women voters tend to vote for the Democratic candidate. Their focus is on health, education, Medicare, and Social Security. Women are nowhere as obsessed as men with saving nickels on electricity or going around locking doors. Those are the kinds of details, however, that dads pass on to their sons.

Our parties, echoing the society that gave rise to them, seem each to have a gender identity. We have the Democratic party that backs the teachers' unions, cares for our education and our health care and sees that grandparents receive their Social Security and Medicare. We have the Republican party that backs big Pentagon budgets, protects the rights of gun owners, backs stiff sentences for criminals, and cuts taxes. We have a "mommy" party and a "daddy" party, each servicing its constituent voters.

AIDS in Africa

Father Angelo D'Agostino, a Jesuit priest, opened Nairobi's Nyumbani Orphanage for HIV-positive children in 1981 when he saw so many HIV-positive children being turned away by other orphanages. Today he is housing and caring for seventy-plus orphans while getting daily medication, clothing, and food to hundreds more who live in surrounding areas.

Kathy, our kids, and I visited Father Dag, as he's known, in summer 1999.

In treating, feeding, raising, and cheering these kids, who range from newborns to teenagers, this seventy-three-year-old Jesuit priest from Providence, Rhode Island, knows that he swims in a roiling sea of need. Sub-Saharan Africa has the highest density of AIDS cases in the world. In Kenya there will be 150,000 HIV-positive orphans by next year. There might be another 200,000 who are not born HIV-positive, but since their mothers died of AIDS, they will live under the stigma of the disease; unwanted by their relatives, they will have no place to live.

With all the love and commitment they receive, however, the prognosis for such orphans is brutally predictable. Nyumbani has no way to afford the high-priced drug cocktails developed for those who are HIV-positive.

"Some chemists are threatening to synthesize the drugs," Father Dag speculates. "What would happen if such companies did manufacture and distribute them at an affordable price? Would the American companies sue them?"

In the meantime, this kindly, thoughtful priest, who was an Air Force surgeon, a psychiatrist, and a refugee worker in his previous life, raises what money he can to give scores of children the best, happiest lives possible.

Swaziland, the country where I served in the Peace Corps, has faced the oppression of apartheid on one border, stubborn Portuguese colonialism on another. Today it is staring at a specter more tragic and more deadly: AIDS. The numbers are staggering. Swaziland has just over a million people. A quarter of them are HIV-positive.

"The situation is quite bad," Ambassador to the U.S. Mary Kanya explains. "Swaziland is number three among the sub-Sahara countries hardest hit. In our hospitals, fifty percent of the people are HIV-positive." And the epidemic is not limited to the poor. "It's hit a cross section," she says, offering the sad accounting. "We're losing some of the most productive population of the country.

"For a long time," she continues, "we have been in denial. The people have been unable to accept the problem. We looked at AIDS as a foreign problem, involving white people, foreign people. Secondly, we saw it as a problem for homosexuals, which we thought was not really a problem for us. Then, when it hit Africa, people looked at AIDS as a problem to the north and east. When it made it to Zimbabwe, we thought it was a problem that was on the other side of the Limpopo [the river separating Zimbabwe from South Africa]."

Like Zimbabwe, Botswana, and other countries in southern Africa, Swaziland is now suffering the full force of the AIDS virus. Life expectancy, which had risen for twenty years, has reverted to its colonial-era standard.

While Ambassador Kanya admits that the "denial is not yet over" in her country, her people clearly are waking up to the AIDS horror, and talking openly about it.

So is the world. In the last year of his vice-presidency, speaking at the United Nations, Al Gore noted the dire statistic that more people will die from this disease in the coming decade than from all the wars of the twentieth century.

Seventeen million dead! Twenty-five million mortally wounded!

If Europe were hit with such ghastly casualties, would America be sitting on the sidelines? If the lands of white America's roots — England, Ireland, Germany, Italy, Poland — faced a global predator capable of such horror, would we avert our glance?

You, the reader: As in 1914 and 1939, this country would be hot with debate: What should we do? How could we best help our friends fight this murderous fiend?

I speak, for those still unaware, not of Europe at the advent of World War I or II but of sub-Saharan Africa at the outbreak of World War III. What will America do this time? Will we wait, as we did in the years before Pearl Harbor, hoping the danger might be arrested somewhere beyond our shores?

Secretary of State Colin Powell has spoken wisely: "AIDS is a national security problem. It is a devastating problem in sub-Saharan Africa. Millions of people are at risk. Millions of people will die no matter what we do. This creates a major problem for Africa and other parts of the world where AIDS is spreading. It is a pandemic. It requires our attention, and Congress has to be generous."

The question is whether President Bush's strategies will apply this "Powell doctrine" as they are morally bound to. Can we show the muscle to fight AIDS in Africa the same way we confronted Saddam Hussein in the Persian Gulf? And will it be backed up by a campaign to build the necessary popular support here at home?

So far, the only government battalions fighting on the front lines have been dispatched by the Peace Corps. Intrepid volunteers in South Africa, Lesotho, and neighboring nations are teaching men how to use condoms and women how to resist them when they don't. They are helping the orphans of AIDS victims learn work skills to help ensure their survival. Beyond their assigned jobs, many Peace Corps volunteers are providing care to the HIV-infected themselves.

For Powell and for President Bush, the question is: Who will lead this fight in Africa? If not the United States, this country of huge medical might and historic wealth, then who? And if AIDS in Africa is a threat to our national security, as Powell has determined, who should carry the U.S. banner?

I suggest President Bush's predecessor, William Jefferson Clinton. His new offices in Harlem would give him an excellent command post from which to champion the American campaign against a global menace that is killing in greater numbers and at greater efficiency than Hitler, Tojo, and Mussolini combined.

I began this chapter by saying that the easiest story to report is the expected, popular version of events. The most controversial is the unexpected, when you find out something you didn't expect — or didn't want — to discover.

In 1990 I went to a Spanish bullfight expecting — wanting — to celebrate the spectacle made famous in the English-speaking world by one of its greatest writers. It didn't turn out that way. Yet my report on the day's events produced more reader reaction, pro and con, than any column I've written before or since.

Death in the Afternoon

BARCELONA, JULY 22, 1990. In his famous guide to the Spanish bullfight, *Death in the Afternoon*, Ernest Hemingway wrote of a classic, if tragic, struggle between man and bull.

This is not what I saw here last Sunday at the Plaza de Toros. Expecting to see a one-on-one contest, I witnessed a series of gang attacks on a half-dozen extremely confused animals.

As is the custom, six bulls were killed that Sunday. I saw none die in the quick and dramatic fashion celebrated in *Death in the Afternoon*. I can assure you none died "swaying on his legs before going up in his back with four legs in the air." No, it was different than that.

The bulls killed here in last Sunday's Corida de Toros met their ends neither quickly nor dramatically. The first bull to enter the ring died the fastest. After taking the full length of the matador's sword in his back, the huge animal wandered dismally around the edge of the ring for several minutes before collapsing. It was not clear what reaction was expected from the crowd during this death walk. My own initial impulse, which I did not follow, was to bolt for the exit stairs mouthing my opinion all the way about this pastime the Spanish consider a sport.

I was wrong to judge the bullfight by a single killing. Each of the other five bulls to enter the ring died even more grotesquely than the first. The second to take the matador's blade roamed the full circumference of the ring after being stabbed, all the while spewing blood through his mouth like a fire hose.

The death of the other four bulls was more complicated. Not being in an aficionado, I assumed this was due to the clumsiness of the matadors.

Instead of doing their work with a single thrust, they spent the afternoon sticking as many as three separate swords into their assigned bulls.

Each time the huge wounded animal would run madly for its life like the Saturday morning cartoon character who runs off the cliff but fails to fall because he doesn't look down.

Hemingway was right about one thing. You know nothing of your true reaction to a bullfight until you have seen one of those once-ferocious animals, a first or second or even third sword run clear through him, still managing to challenge the bullfighters surrounding him. You know nothing of your reaction to the bullfighters themselves until you have watched the matador and his coterie of *banderilleros* pursuing and harassing these dying bulls until they can run no more.

Then there is the real dirty work of the modern Spanish bullfight — the coup de grace. This is when one of the *banderilleros* takes out a penknife, stabs the wounded bull between the eyes and then sticks the blade into the animal's ear and gouges him to death as if he were a young boy cutting the core from an apple.

There is something else I saw and learned in the greatly sunny Plaza de Toros Monumental last Sunday.

The bullfight is not, as it is so often advertised in movies and literature, some great heroic test of wits between man and beast. The whole tragedy of the bullfight — the animals charging into the ring, the teasing by the *banderilleros*, the brutal lancing by the mounted picadors, the insertion of the painful *banderillas*, the cape work by the matador and the slow final butchering — is less a one-on-one affair and more a gangland-style execution.

From the time the bull enters the scene he is relentlessly harassed and confused by the *banderilleros*, either standing in the ring itself or teasing him and taunting him from behind.

Even when the matador stood alone in the ring, his *banderilleros* regularly worked to distract the bull. The second the matador got in trouble, every time a bull turned too abruptly toward him or failed to follow his cue, the matador's claque of *banderilleros* would emerge from behind the fence to lure the bull away and their boss to safety.

Even after the sword or several swords had been plunged full-length into the animal, the matador's lieutenants continued to harass and distract the bull.

This confusion and humiliation of the bull gives some support, I suppose, to the tragedy. How much easier it is to butcher a beast once he has been made to look stupid.

But if the bull were so stupid, why is so much effort made to keep him confused throughout this so-called sporting activity? If he is so lacking in basic intelligence, why is the fighting bull kept from the sight of a dismounted man until he enters the ring to be killed in the first place?

And if the bull requires so much effort to be confused and subdued, why is he the worthy object of so much of our torture?

RONALD REAGAN

I first met Ronald Reagan in Speaker O'Neill's ceremonial office. The Secret Service was keeping him there while its dogs sniffed for bombs under the seats on the House floor.

"Welcome, Mr. President, to the room where we plot against you!" I said upon entering.

"Not after six," our guest responded without hesitation. "The Speaker says that here in Washington we're all friends after six!"

Yes, it really happened that way. I was that imprudent and Ronald Reagan was that masterful in taking command.

Like other Hollywood actors, Reagan was a tougher, more on-guard character than one would assume from his breezy public personality. The man you met then was not the beneficiary of his seemingly golden circumstances but rather the chief protector of his own charmed life. He was the combatant who knows, without needing a warning, just when he has entered the enemy's lair.

An hour after my brash greeting, a hundred million Americans turned on their television sets to watch this apparently easygoing fellow with his crease of a grin.

The Ronald Reagan there in the Speaker's room was the guy who had survived his divorce from Jane Wyman, the decline of his movie career, the cancellation of his TV show, and the cruel social downgrading that rides shotgun on such defeats. He was the quick-on-his-feet orator who had defeated Bobby Kennedy in debate before the Oxford Union. He was the no-nonsense boss who fired thirteen thousand striking U.S. air traffic controllers. He was the political street fighter who got up off the dirt to win the 1976 North Carolina primary when nearly everybody counted him for dead. He was the cold-blooded combatant who strode to the podium of the 1976 Republican convention and delivered such a barn-burner it made people wonder what Gerald Ford, the party nominee, was doing on the stage.

Like millions who watched television in the 1950s, I had gotten to know and like Reagan during his eight years hosting the old *General Electric Theater.* Every Sunday night at nine, he would warmly greet his huge prime-time audience and introduce the forthcoming story. Occasionally, he himself would star. Like most baby boomers I knew nothing of his earlier movie career. Only later would I learn that he had played the Notre Dame football hero George Gipp in *Knute Rockne: All American.* To me, Ronald Reagan was simply the guy I shared my Sunday evenings with. Like Sid Caesar and Steve Allen and Johnny Carson, he was one of those TV people about whom one could say I forged a bond. I think millions of people did.

This is where the professionals blew it. To Pat Brown, the Democratic California governor Reagan unseated in 1966, Ronald Reagan was just a "B-movie actor," a guy who turned out serviceable second-rate movies for the double features people often went to see before television came along.

I think Tip O'Neill, for all his insider's street smarts, shared this miscalculation. He and the others didn't see the brilliant outsider's game Reagan was playing. His Democratic rivals saw Reagan simply as a minor-league movie star, when actually television had turned him into something more. He wasn't some guy playing a character in the movies, but rather one we had invited into our homes each Sunday night. Looking back on his defeat years later, Pat

Brown would realize that in the voter's mind, Reagan was always one of "us," while he was always one of "them."

Ronald Reagan came across as the classic American populist challenging the halls of entrenched authority. He, the kid who'd grown up believing in the New Deal, was now the soft-spoken revolutionary opposed to big government. He spoke not only for Republicans, but for all Americans, optimistic about what man can do if left to be free. He may never have played "Mr. Smith" but he out-acted Jimmy Stewart in the long run — which is to say, he got to live the part.

That's both the medium and the message that the big boys never caught onto when they were out doing what Reagan liked to call "the rubber chicken circuit." Once people stopped going to meetings in the evening and started watching TV, men like Ronald Reagan became a lot more familiar than full-time old school politicians such as Pat Brown and Tip O'Neill. The paint-by-the-numbers Democrats never saw him coming because too many of them obviously never watched television. They led their people into dismissing him as a "B-movie actor." That self-delusion turned out to be suicidal.

Another fact overlooked by his critics was that Ronald Reagan was not just a great "communicator." From the beginning, Reagan was a man with a cause. I remember the time he opened *GE Theater* by saying that the story he was about to introduce mattered to him personally. It concerned a woman who had been hoodwinked into joining a Communist front group. Discovering that the group was getting its cues from Moscow, the woman had turned informant. She became a double agent. At the urging of the FBI, she posed as a member of the leftist group and did reconnaissance work, yet as a result suffered daily the contempt of her neighbors.

HERE'S WHAT I REALLY THINK: I think that Ronald Reagan's self-styled "citizen-politician" pose was bogus. He had been running for president since the day he left *GE Theater* in 1962. His speech for Barry Goldwater in 1964 was really the kick-off to his own run. His campaign for California governor in 1966 was a career arrow aimed directly at the White House. Why would a guy with Reagan's philosophy want to be a government administrator? After just a year in Sacramento, he launched his '68 presidential race, and that was that.

But it was too soon. Ronald Reagan was,

for the first time, up against a politician who displayed a few tricks of his own. Through an alliance with South Carolina's Strom Thurmond, Richard Nixon outflanked Reagan in the area of the country where his philosophy commanded its utmost appeal, the conservative South. Then, with Nixon broken by Watergate, Reagan tried once again, but was thwarted by party loyalty to Nixon's handpicked successor, Gerald Ford. Finally, in 1980, on the third try, the Gipper proved to be at the top of his game.

Those of us working for Jimmy Carter didn't know what hit us. A hint of it had come in Reagan's speech accepting the Republican nomination. After a brief reminder of the Carter administration's sorry economic record, the newly minted candidate switched to sarcasm: "Can anyone look at the record of this administration and say, 'Well done!'? Or at the state of our economy when the Carter administration took office with where we are today and say, 'Keep up the good work!'?"

Then came the cavalry attack. "Can anyone look at our reduced standing in the world today and say, 'Let's have four more years of this'?"

President Carter launched his fall reelection campaign at a huge Labor Day picnic in Alabama. As the assigned speechwriter, I was anxious to see how the event would play on the evening news. Peeking into a Georgetown restaurant, I realized to my surprise what we were up against. There on the TV screen above the bar was Ronald Reagan, charismatic as hell, standing in shirtsleeves on a piece of overlooked real estate in New Jersey. Behind him loomed an icon of treasured American myth — the Statue of Liberty. I smelled trouble in River City. We weren't running against a Republican; we were running against the republic!

What were the secrets to his great success? I can think of three strengths he carried with him into the political arena. They could only be labeled as secret if you were someone relying on the Democrats' talking points.

1. Ronald Reagan knew why he wanted to be president.
2. He knew how to talk to real people.
3. He could describe his feelings about our country invoking the spirit most Americans share but have trouble expressing.

Every cab driver knew that Reagan wanted to beat the Communists abroad and to cut government and taxes at home. When

Reagan spoke about "the boys" who stormed Normandy or the astronauts lost in the *Challenger*, he tapped into the deepest sentiments of his hero-worshipping compatriots. While he may never have fought in World War II, he evoked its aura with greater success than anyone who had ever lived on K-rations. The only times he got into real trouble as president were occasions when neither Communism nor big government came into play. The decision to deploy the Marines in Lebanon in 1983 and the arms-for-hostages deal of three years later were two situations when his worldview failed him.

The troubling truth is that this impressive American leader was just as compelling when he was fudging. He recited movie dialog as if it were real life when he told Israeli prime minister Yitzhak Shamir and Nazi-chaser Simon Wiesenthal that he had photographed the death camps for the Army Signal Corps.

It was a stunning experience to hear Ronald Reagan say so confidently, in his TV debate with Carter, what I knew to be a lie. For years I'd heard him speak against such contributory programs as Social Security and Medicare.

Indeed, Reagan had fought Medicare at

the time of its creation just as Republicans before him had fought Social Security. Now he was making the shameless claim that he, Ronald Reagan, had championed creation of a federal program to get medical care to retired Americans.

But, even when Carter was right and Reagan was wrong in their debate, all people remember from the exchange and indeed from the entire evening was the challenger's brutal put-away line: "There you go again, Mr. President." With those six withering words, the challenger reduced the incumbent to a desperate, sweating hack clinging to a great office he was no longer strong enough to fill.

Reagan entered the pantheon of mythical American heroes — Casey at the bat, John Henry, Paul Bunyan — with the grace and humor he exhibited after the assassination attempt on him in March of his inaugural year. "Honey, I forgot to duck," he told wife Nancy. And, "I hope you're all Republicans," he kidded the doctors as he was wheeled into the operating room. An actor who had spent decades playing heroes suddenly had transcended the back lot and its illusions.

Where presidents since Kennedy were willing to coexist with the USSR, Reagan demanded that Gorbachev tear down the Berlin Wall. When that happened in November 1989 on President George H. W. Bush's watch, I saluted the American president whose bright-eyed and brisk sentiments had helped to trigger the demolition. "This is the week I miss Ronald Reagan," I wrote in my newspaper column. "He would have known what to say."

HERE'S WHAT I REALLY THINK: I think that the man who played George Gipp in *Knute Rockne: All American* never stopped trying to reinvent the forward pass. Why couldn't the bold play that won on the cinematic football field work on the U.S. economy? Instead of endless trench warfare over budget cuts, Reagan would surprise his rivals with some razzle-dazzle: a big tax cut. Instead of competing with the Soviets on how many missiles we could deploy at each other, he'd commission a missile shield that would render their missiles irrelevant.

Did the Reagan policies work? Politically, yes. Getting Congress to cut taxes helped stimulate the "morning in America" economic boom of 1983–84. Threatening Gorbachev with a missile shield, something his engineers could never build but ours might, may have caused the Soviet leader to call off the Cold War. But there was a considerable cost. Taken together, the 1981 tax cut and the big hike in strategic weapons spending produced huge annual deficits and quadrupled the national debt.

The smiling myth that was the Reagan presidency produced two benefits. The first was for the Republican party. For instance, when the Democrats decided to make the 1994 election a referendum comparing the early Clinton record with the Reagan record, they lost both houses of Congress for the first time in half a century. Like Paul Bunyan, he'll always be there, towering above the landscape of lesser figures.

The other beneficiary of the myth was Ronald Reagan himself. Early in his movie career he played Secret Service agent Brass Bancroft in a series of four films. One of the kids to love those movies was a boy named Jerry Parr. When he grew up Jerry decided that he, too, wanted to be a Secret Service agent. In fact, he made his career in the Secret Service and rose to become chief of the presidential protection detail during Reagan's administration. When the shooting started that day in front of the Washington Hilton, a gutsy, quick-witted Jerry Parr was there to shove the critically wounded president into the car. It was Parr who jumped into the backseat on top of him to keep the deranged John Hinckley from getting him with a second bullet. It was the same chief presidential bodyguard who ordered that the driver race to George Washington University Hospital in just over ten minutes, just time enough to save Brass Bancroft's life.

That story is typical of Reagan's good fortune in life, which only abandoned him when the effects of Alzheimer's disease overtook him. That, too, he took with grace. He wrote a last letter to the country in 1994 in which he expressed his profound belief in its future. He wrote, "I now begin the journey that will lead me into the sunset of my life. I know that for America there will always be a bright dawn ahead."

Ronald Reagan did not "win" the Cold War but he belongs in the roster of those who did. That list began with President Harry Truman, who drew the line on Soviet expansion in Europe with the Marshall Plan and the Truman Doctrine. It includes all the other Cold War presidents of both parties who contained Communism until it could destroy itself. What set Reagan apart was his insistence that there be a winner and a loser.

Chapter Nine

Worldly Wisdom

If you add it up, I've spent thirty years studying politicians. In academic terms, that's at least sixty semesters of real-life political science. In *Hardball*, which I wrote in 1988, you can find some of the basics. In this chapter I now offer three giant precepts as a kind of advanced seminar. They will get you where you want to get; better yet, they will help you be who you want to be. They constitute a user's manual for the politics of personal ambition.

Show Up!

NINETY PERCENT OF LIFE IS SHOWING UP.
WOODY ALLEN

To win the game, you've got to get in it. Regardless of what you want to do with your life, in order to do it well, you've got to go to where the game is being played and get involved. This is pretty basic stuff, I went to grammar school with a kid named Jimmy Schuhl. He was the most popular kid in the class and, of course, good at sports. I remember him once explaining how he had become so good. Every afternoon he would go to the neighborhood playground and stand alongside the court while the older kids played basketball. Whenever the ball went out of bounds, he'd run and get it and throw it back in. Each night, as it got close to supper, one of the older kids would have to bail out. To even up the sides, one of them would yell, "Hey you, kid, want to play?" It's as simple as that. "Hey you, kid, want to play?"

A quarter-century ago, author/actor/law school professor Ben Stein codified this rule of life in *The Wall Street Journal.* He called it "Bunkhouse Logic." It's one newspaper column I've never forgotten.

You most likely know Stein as the host of *Win Ben Stein's Money* on cable's Comedy Central. But you may not know you watched him play the nerdy teacher in *Ferris Bueller's Day Off,* or that maddening slowpoke in front of the airport check-in line when Nicolas Cage was trying to save his wife from James Caan in *Honeymoon in Vegas.*

In the column "Bunkhouse Logic" Stein wrote about the kids with whom he'd gone to Montgomery Blair High School in suburban Washington, D.C. Most of them were ambitious and driven, and like so many teenagers, many who dreamed of being rich and famous ended up taking safe career routes — first to law school, then to some big firm, corporation, or bureaucracy. Only two succeeded early: Goldie Hawn and Carl Bernstein.

Goldie had the guts to go for glory. A drama major at Washington's American University, she one day decided to hitch a ride to New York. There she got a gig dancing at the New York World's Fair. Later she used her dancer's skills as a go-go girl on weekends while she tried out for shows. Working her way to Los Angeles and subsequently onto television, she met a producer. He asked her to audition for a new show called *Rowan & Martin's Laugh-In*. Instantly, she became a TV star. Cast as Walter Matthau's too young girlfriend in *Cactus Flower*, she was soon a movie star. She's made countless films since, including classics like *Private Benjamin*.

Carl Bernstein's route to success was shorter. He eschewed college. Wanting to be a reporter, he went straight to work at

The Washington Post. He was in the city room when some burglars were arrested at the Democratic National Committee headquarters. *Why?* he wondered. His curiosity and his tenacity drove he and Bob Woodward to score the biggest scoop of the twentieth century: the Watergate cover-up.

"You cannot win if you're not at the table," Stein deduced. It's the best, most basic advice I have ever come across. Practicing what he preached, Ben now boasts his own TV show. "I can't believe Ben Stein is a star!" Goldie Hawn told me at dinner after appearing on *Hardball* last year.

Getting that seat at the table accomplishes several things. It's how you (a) meet people. It's how you (b) learn the business. And it's how you (c) put yourself in position to be dealt a winning hand, to be there when the lightning strikes.

It's not who you know, I've discovered, it's who you get to know. Former New York senator Daniel Patrick Moynihan said that getting a prized West Wing office during his Nixon White House service "meant I could piss standing next to White House Chief-of-Staff H. R. Haldeman."

It's how I got on the editorial staff of my high-school newspaper. It's how I got my first job with Senator Frank Moss, became a professional staffer on the Senate Budget Committee, a top aide to Tip O'Neill, and a nationally syndicated columnist and bureau chief for the *San Francisco Examiner*. I was there when the job opened up.

There's a false assumption out there that talent will always be recognized. Just get good at something and the world will beat a path to your door. Don't believe it. The world is not checking in with us to see what skills we've picked up, what idea we've concocted, what dreams we carry in our hearts. When a job opens up, whether it's in the chorus line or on the assembly line, it goes to the person standing there. It goes to the eager beaver the boss sees when he looks up from his work, the pint-sized kid standing at courtside waiting for one of the older boys to head home for dinner. "Hey, kid, wanna play?"

This isn't only about being a movie star or a renowned investigative journalist. It's about getting where you want to get in life. If you want to be a lawyer, get into the best school you can or you can get into the worst school. Just find some desperate place in obscurity that can't fill its rolls. Either way, you will get your law degree.

This is the logic that motivated me in 1971 as I knocked on two hundred doors on

Capitol Hill before getting my first job in politics.

The more I study the careers of successful people the more I see this pattern. Here are two examples I always think of:

Ernest Hemingway wanted to be a writer. He went to the place where writers gathered, the Left Bank. There he met the people, especially F. Scott Fitzgerald, who would encourage him in his writing and recommend him to their editors back in New York. He settled himself in what he would later describe as "the town best organized for a writer to write," a city Gertrude Stein said "was where the twentieth century was."

Secretary of State Colin Powell also put himself in the right place. "There may be one moment in our lives we can look back on later and say that, for good or ill, it was the turning point. For me that day came in November 1971." It was the day the thirty-five-year-old army officer was told to apply for a White House fellowship.

It was his service as a White House Fellow that brought Powell, a self-described poor minority kid from the South Bronx, into daily personal contact with the people who would open doors for him. Without that access, Powell never would have achieved his great success.

HERE'S WHAT I REALLY THINK: I think that in order to win the game, you first need a seat at the table.

Ask!

IF YOU KNOCK LONG ENOUGH AND LOUD ENOUGH AT THE GATE YOU ARE BOUND TO WAKE UP SOMEBODY.
HENRY WADSWORTH LONGFELLOW

If you want something, ask for it. Some people aren't going to like the cut of your jib. But those who do will change your life. They will open doors for you. They will invest in you — if you're fortunate, not just once, but repeatedly.

My experience in the Peace Corps in Africa is a case in point. Each day, I had to ask Swazi traders — people vastly different from myself — to trust me and do things for me. Thanks to that experience I came to Washington well prepared to meet perfect strangers and immediately ask them to hire me. I described earlier how I had knocked on two hundred doors on Capitol Hill before I got the job that changed everything. It was then I noticed how every door that was opened for me was opened by someone on the inside. The secret, as Longfellow suggests, is to knock long enough and loud enough that someone can hear you.

Not everybody is going to buy your act. The good news is that there will be people who say "yes." It packs enormous impact. It takes only one strike to transform a prospector into a gold miner, only one "yes" to turn a proposal into a marriage.

Thanks to a mutual friend, Bob Schiffer, Hendrik Hertzberg and I became friends when we both came to the Carter White House in 1977. Rik, a former *New Yorker* staff writer, had one of the prestigious posts, presidential speechwriter. He got to eat in the White House mess, consort with other top sides, and most important, write the words the president would say. When Rik was promoted to chief speechwriter, leaving his former position vacant, I asked Rik if I could fill it. Thanks to him, and a successful tryout, I got the job.

There is a magic that results when a person invests in you. If you're an investment for someone, there's a bond to be honored by both of you. I owe not just my speechwriting job to Rik but my start in journalism. As editor of *The New Republic* he ran a healthy number of my articles in the years after we left the White House.

In late 1986, when Tip O'Neill was

nearing retirement, I went to visit Howard Stringer, president of CBS News. After a warm get-acquainted chat, I asked my British-born host if he'd consider creating a position under him similar to the deputy position Timothy Russert, a former aide to Senator Daniel Patrick Moynihan, had carved out with NBC News president Larry Grossman. (It was not the last time I would see Tim as a positive role model.) Stringer replied that CBS didn't have the means to make the big budgetary commitment that a Russert-type position required. He said I should instead consider going on air.

A year later, after I found myself hired as Washington bureau chief of the *San Francisco Examiner*, I returned to take him up on his suggestion. Immediately, Stringer took me down the hall to meet David Corvo, at the time the executive producer of *CBS This Morning*. I brought along a videotape of an appearance I had just made on ABC's *Good Morning America*, discussing a recent *New Republic* article I'd written on the 1988 presidential candidates. Soon after, David began inviting me onto CBS to do political commentary.

Hardball also had its genesis in a request. A decade ago I had dinner in Beverly Hills with Joe McGinniss, author of *The Selling of the President* and some highly successful books on real-life murder cases. He was working on a book about Senator Edward Kennedy and wanted my thoughts. Afterward, Joe said he was having drinks at the Four Seasons with a guy he thought I'd like. When he said it was Roger Ailes, it was a name I immediately recognized. He was the media genius who had worked for Richard Nixon and Ronald Reagan.

Ailes had concocted the senior George Bush's lethal ad campaign against 1988 Democratic presidential candidate Michael Dukakis and his Massachusetts prison "furlough" program. McGinniss's hunch was right: Roger and I hit it off from the first, and I decided to stay in touch. Whenever I came to New York I would look him up. We talked politics and, eventually, of someday putting together a fast-paced TV show. That day came in 1994 when Roger was named head of CNBC and the new NBC cable network called "America's Talking." I asked Roger if I could do a show. He said yes.

When you ask someone for help, you are implicitly asking him to place a bet on you. The more people you get to bet on you, the larger your network of investors and the shorter your odds. And it illustrates, also,

Ben Franklin's wisdom, advice that may seem counterintuitive: "If you want to make a friend, let someone do you a favor." Many people hesitate to ask for help. They see it as an admission of weakness. But this do-it-yourself mentality can be lethal. It can limit and isolate a contender, denying him allies. People spend their whole lives resisting having others do favors for them. In doing so, they forfeit not only the gift directly offered, but something far more important: the power that comes from receiving.

Never forget the basic accounting principle at work here: an account receivable is an asset.

Once that guy across the table or woman across the dance floor says "yes," it creates an instant bond. Just as rejection admits a chasm, acceptance begins a communion. The people who get favors are the folks with the nerve to ask for them — and keep asking! Persistence has its rewards.

Take Jack McMacken, a guy who goes to my church. When he was at Notre Dame, he applied to Yale Law School, the most selective in the country. When he inquired at the dean of admissions' office about getting in for an interview, his secretary said Yale Law didn't grant interviews. But he kept calling the secretary, chatting with her about his desire to attend the school. When the acceptances went out, Jack found himself wait-listed. Again, he called the admissions office and asked for an interview. This time, the dean of admissions' secretary relented. Although it was not the school's practice, she invited Jack McMacken to fly to New Haven, which he did, through a blinding, terrifying snowstorm, to meet her boss, the dean of admissions. Jack graduated from Yale Law three years later.

Another illustration is Steve Case, today chairman of AOL Time Warner. The young Case was a visionary, seeing the opportunities of the Internet before anyone else. But that's not where he got his start. Fresh out of college, Case was rejected by every business school he applied to. Knowing that Procter & Gamble was a great training ground for marketing, he applied to work there and was rejected. He flew back to Cincinnati, P&G's headquarters, at his own expense, and talked his way into another interview. Case was hired as an assistant brand manager.

And he kept it up. In the early days of AOL, when the company was known as Quantum, Case flew to California to try to convince Apple Computer to let Quantum develop their online service. To show his interest, he showed up every day for three months. Finally, Apple agreed to the deal.

HERE'S WHAT I REALLY THINK: The passport to getting what you want is very often the simple, courageous act of asking for it. When you get rejected, when you get that "no!" right in your face, remember that "no" is better than no answer. It saves time — which is what you need if you are going to get rejected nine times out of ten. And all that means is that you have to ask ten times.

Believe!

CONSCIOUSNESS PRECEDES BEING AND NOT THE OTHER WAY AROUND, AS MARXISTS CLAIM.

VACLAV HAVEL

Ideals count, particularly the ideal you hold of yourself.

"It was clear from our very first meeting that Ron Reagan was in politics out of passionate belief," former British prime minister Margaret Thatcher said. It's hard to argue with that assessment, whatever your country or politics.

Ideals matter. Geza Jeszenszky believed that "freedom is contagious." That young man I interviewed at the Brandenburg Gate certainly knew what freedom is. "Talking to you," he said. Five years later in Cape Town it was the democratic ideal that caused a line of voters to stretch from one horizon to another.

Ideas matter, too, especially one's own ideas. One has to know one's own taste and follow it where it leads.

When my family began spending summers in Ocean City, New Jersey, I came across a local kid who was totally caught up in pop culture. He argued that Marlon Brando was a better actor than Cary Grant, a point on which I disagreed. He knew about this new singer who was performing in front of largely black audiences in a tough part of Atlantic City named Ray Charles.

The kid's name was Kurt Loder. You know him today as the guy who does the commentary on MTV.

It's like me and politics. People who knew me in college remember me as the guy forever arguing politics down in the cafeteria. Congressman Ed Markey, a Boston College grad, often kids me that I get paid five nights a week "just for going down to the Holy Cross caf."

More important people with big ideas have changed history. Here are just a few of my favorites:

Thomas Paine, a recent English immigrant to the North American colonies, wrote *Common Sense* in January 1776. Arguing the case for independence, it sold a half million copies. Six months later, the Continental Congress declared Paine's idea to the world.

In 1852, the wife of a Bowdoin College professor wrote *Uncle Tom's Cabin, or Life Among the Lowly*. It sold three million copies. Harriet Beecher Stowe had made slavery an issue that transcended states' rights — in her hands it became a human issue. "You're the little lady who made this big war," Abraham Lincoln said on meeting her in 1862.

A century later, Rachel Carson, author of *Silent Spring*, alerted the world to the dangers of environmental pollution. And Ralph Nader began the consumer movement with *Unsafe at Any Speed*, his muckraking book on auto safety.

I have often mentioned Holy Cross on *Hardball* and not simply out of loyalty. I'm fortunate to have had a Jesuit education, since it asks not how but *why*. I'm proud to have graduated from a college that has turned out a stream of such notable crusaders of both Left and Right. My fellow alumni include Michael Harrington, author of *The Other America*, credited with inspiring the War on Poverty of the 1960s, and Supreme Court justice Clarence Thomas, a proponent of the value of self-reliance. The country's top lawyer of his era, Edward Bennett Williams, insisted on the right of the most despised — from Joseph McCarthy to John Hinckley — to a strong defense in court.

Holy Cross graduate Philip Berrigan committed civil disobedience, and cheerfully paid its civil price, for his opposition to the Vietnam War and what he views as the country's excessive militarism. "It's much better to make a statement with one's life," he once said, "than with one's mouth." Pennsylvania governor Bob Casey, a liberal to his core, opposed abortion to his last breath, even as his party tried to gag him. Former Health, Education, and Welfare secretary Joseph Califano gave up a lucrative legal practice to wage a crusade against drug abuse. As director of the National Institute of Allergy and Infectious Diseases, Dr. Anthony Fauci has spent years leading the struggle for a cure to AIDS.

The lives of these men all bear the same mark. All understand how an ideal can be a beacon. All are toughened veterans of that

Jesuit education. As Harrington put it, "From the time I was a little kid the Church said your life is not something you are supposed to fritter away. Your life is a trust to something more important than yourself." I'd bet that every one of these men — the antiwar Berrigan, the prolife liberal Casey, the steadfast conservative Thomas, the civil libertarian Williams, the anti-AIDS crusader Fauci — would recognize that sentiment as his own. I do.

If there is a messianic quality to such lives, there is also an accompanying touch of vanity — and I recognize that as well.

CHAPTER TEN

PLAYING HARDBALL

THERE'S NOTHING I LOVE AS MUCH AS A
GOOD FIGHT.

FRANKLIN D. ROOSEVELT

Dad used to say that a politician was a guy
who stood out on the corner and yelled. His
definition was inspired by the young pair of
aristocratic Ivy Leaguers, Richardson
Dilworth and Joseph Clark, who cleaned up
Philadelphia politics in the early 1950s. At
lunchtime this heroic duo would stand at the
corner of Broad and Chestnut streets and rail
against the "drones in City Hall" and
demand reform. Because of them, the people
of Philadelphia voted to end eighty-seven
years of rule by the corrupt old Republican
machine.

This is what I try to do five nights a week
on national television. I interview the
people who run the country, hit them with

224

hard questions, and challenge them to give real answers. If it's too boisterous, too loud for you, let me leave you with a warning: Democracy is a noisy business. It's when it gets quiet up here on the national stage that you should begin to worry.

It's also my experience that the cacophony that you hear coming from Washington is often the echo of a real division in the country. As famed newspaper editor William Allen White wrote, "In no other country in the world is aspiration so definite a part of life as it is in America. The most precious gift God has given to this land is not its great riches of soil and forest and land but the *divine discontent* planted deeply in the hearts of the American people."

I don't pretend to be an idle bystander. As my friend John McLaughlin once noted, I'm a *tummler,* the Yiddish term for the guy at the old Catskills resorts whose job it was to stir things up on a rainy day. That's me on *Hardball.* I'm the one who's supposed to get people engaged, get them into the act. More often than not, I'm engaged already. It's my belief that if someone has no passions, he or she has no business either running for office, standing on a downtown corner holding a bullhorn, or hosting a political talk show.

Somebody recently described *Hardball* as "just entertainment." Guess what? I'll live with the qualifying adjective if I can get that noun. Those who think the category "entertainer" belittles my work should recall Bob Dylan. He made a point of saying his singing was just that. My dad makes the distinction in this way: He calls *Hardball* a "show" rather than a program.

I'll admit it. I love it when I can zing some guest for using "talking points."

A farmer named Steve wrote me saying, "Been watching you now for awhile. Always marvel at the enjoyment you seem to get out of it. You obviously like doing what you're doing. I appreciate your even-handedness in your approach and ability to keep it on the subject even if you have to cut some hot-aired person off."

You're right, Steve. Not only am I having fun, but I want the *Hardball* guests and viewers to have fun as well.

As for those invited to be on the show, here is what I'd like you to bring along with you.

1. Facts. I want people to learn something watching *Hardball.*
2. Spontaneity. Please leave the talking points back at the office.

3. Honesty. When the other side nails you, admit it.

4. Feistiness. Why should the host be all alone in this?

5. Laughter. This isn't the Inquisition. No one really gets hurt. In fact, guests usually want to come back for more.

My goal is to cover the country's politics. My main weakness as a journalist covering them is that I love politicians. Remember that congressman who walked across the chamber to ask his political adversary what he was up to for the weekend and to say hello to his wife for him? That, to me, is democracy. If Jefferson or Adams or Madison could have seen that moment on the floor of Congress, they would have seen their dream fulfilled. It symbolizes the democratic republic for which they struggled.

I have a particular affection for the House of Representatives and the members I worked with all those years. That is, despite the fact that many now treat me as an outsider. I know that they are angry with me for being so tough on President Clinton and other Democrats. Some even saw my movement into journalism in 1987 as a betrayal. The fact is, we are in different professions now. My job is to report on what they do, not sing their praises.

But I also know deep in my soul that I have never been an institutionalist or "one of the boys." That explains my untrendy empathy for Richard Milhous Nixon, the man. But most important, it allows me to watch political events through the eyes of an outsider. I like it that way because it helps me be what I have to be: independent.

I well recall that big empty 747 I took from Heathrow to New York on my way home from the Peace Corps thirty years ago. The cavernous coach cabin was empty except for a few bored, out-of-sight flight attendants. *Citizen Kane*, Orson Welles's masterpiece, was playing on the forward bulkhead. I remember when the title character, an emerging newspaper baron based upon William Randolph Hearst, is being attacked from both sides. A labor boss calls him a "fascist," while the rich financier dismisses him as a "Communist."

But "there was another voice," the narrator intones. Then we see the words: "I am what I have always been: an American." Below them is the signature of Charles Foster Kane.

I used to think that the great Kane character was merely dodging the question with that answer. Today I think he was saying exactly what I would say. Am I a liberal or a conservative? I can give you the formula if you want it: I've got a conservative gut, a liberal, tolerant mind, and a heart — which breaks the tie. But I'll settle for what Kane had to say on the subject. By reading the previous chapters, you know that I believe it.

Now that I've finished writing the book, I can once again enjoy Washington. I have loved it since my first visit with my parents and two of my brothers in 1954. I love my job, as you can see. But I also love this city. I am especially fond of driving home at night past the great monuments to Lincoln and Jefferson, often looking across the Potomac to the lawn of Robert E. Lee's mansion and that little twinkle of light guarding the grave of John F. Kennedy.

How seductive politics can be. But how much greater is this feeling of being an American. That's the real pull of this place. Despite all the statues of generals on horse-back, Washington is a city of elected civilians. We build those monuments to the great presidents, not so much to honor the past as to goad the current president. If the dream is to endure, we must live it. If that means making a little noise, I say, that's all in a day's work.

ABOUT THE AUTHOR

Chris Matthews hosts *Hardball with Chris Matthews* Monday through Friday at 8 and 11 p.m. on CNBC and at 7 p.m. on MSNBC.

Matthews is a frequent commentator on NBC's *Today* and the regular substitute anchor on NBC's *Weekend Today*. He is a nationally syndicated columnist for the *San Francisco Chronicle*.

He is the author of *Hardball* (1988) and *Kennedy & Nixon* (1996), which was selected for *The Reader's Digest* "Today's Best Nonfiction."

A graduate of Holy Cross, Matthews did graduate work in economics at the University of North Carolina and was a trade development adviser with the U.S. Peace Corps in the southern African nation of Swaziland.

In 1987, Matthews joined the *San Francisco Examiner*, where he served as Washington Bureau Chief for thirteen years. Prior to entering journalism, Matthews served as a presidential speechwriter for

Jimmy Carter and a top aide to House Speaker Thomas P. O'Neill, Jr.

Matthews covered the opening of the Berlin Wall, the first all-races election in South Africa, and the historic peace referendum in Northern Ireland and the Republic of Ireland. In 1997 and 1998, his research in the National Archives produced a series of *Examiner* scoops on the Nixon presidential tapes. He has twice received the *Washington Post*'s "Crystal Ball" award for his successful predictions of U.S. presidential elections.

One of the highlights of *Hardball*'s coverage of the 2000 election was the "Hardball College Tour," which featured town meetings at Harvard, Penn, Clemson, USC, Michigan State, St. Anselm, and Winona State University.

Mr. Matthews has received honorary doctoral degrees from St. Leo University, Loyola College (Maryland), Niagara University, Fontbonne College, Beaver College, the New England School of Law, Anna Maria College, and Chestnut Hill College. He has given the Marsh Lecture at Shenandoah University, the Hanify-Howland Lecture at Holy Cross, the Churchill Lecture at Salisbury State University, and the Kelly-Weiss Lecture at the University of Notre Dame. He serves on the International Board of Trustees of the Churchill Center. This fall he is a Visiting Fellow at Harvard's John F. Kennedy Institute of Politics.

Matthews is married to Kathleen Matthews, news anchor for the ABC affiliate in Washington, D.C. They have three children: Michael, Thomas, and Caroline.